A Cooper Union Forum Book

AMERICA FACES THE NUCLEAR AGE

AMERICA FACES

THE NUCLEAR AGE

A Cooper Union Forum

EDITED BY

JOHNSON E. FAIRCHILD

AND

DAVID LANDMAN

SHERIDAN HOUSE • NEW YORK

ACKNOWLEDGEMENTS

This book was made possible by the cooperation of several organizations and by the help and labor of many people. The editors wish particularly to thank the Joint Industry Board of the Electrical Industry of New York, The Cooper Union for the Advancement of Science and Art, the Consolidated Edison Company of New York, and these individuals: John E. Kenton and Charles E. Hoppin who gave so generously of their advice, Helen L. Goring who prepared the bibliography, the patient publisher Lee Furman, and Anne Kassow who performed so many great and little chores to help transform an idea into a book.

J.E.F.
D.L.

PUBLISHER'S NOTE

Dr. Richard F. Humphreys is president of The Cooper Union for the Advancement of Science and Art. A nuclear physicist, he taught at Yale ten years before going to the Armour Research Foundation of Illinois Institute of Technology where he served as assistant director and vice president for technical development.

Professor Johnson E. Fairchild is director of adult education at The Cooper Union and chairman of The Cooper Union Forum. A social geographer, he was formerly dean at Hunter College of the City of New York.

David Landman, assistant to the president at The Cooper Union, was chairman of the conference: "The Electrical Industry Faces the Nuclear Age." For fifteen years he did free-lance reporting for various national magazines.

PREFACE

The events at Alamogordo, Hiroshima and Nagasaki near the end of World War II stunned the peoples of
the world. There could no longer be any doubt of the
destructive power of nuclear fission, but the obverse of
the coin—man's capability for using fission as a benevolent contribution to society—was less easy to decipher. The
most promising application for the gain of mankind was
that a vast quantity of relatively low-temperature heat is
generated by controlled fission with an almost minuscule
mass of fuel. The possibility of economic nuclear power
was thus suggested.

The operative word of this phrase is "economic" and today it is still an open question whether the adjective is
appropriate. Traditionally the economics of industrial
processes is based on experience and technological development, but too little time has elapsed for either of these
factors to be a reliable indicator to the company assessing
the wisdom of investing tens of millions of dollars in
nuclear power.

Nonetheless, the curve of demand by this power-hungry
nation virtually guarantees the exploitation of the nucleus
as a source of energy, nor do we have any leisure time to

[13

get the job started. Experience, and the improvements devolving from it, must be had now, not ten or twenty years from now. Not only the economics of nuclear-power generation must be established, but the techniques of protecting the public from the hazards of radiation—techniques which *are* well established and based on experience —must merit the full confidence of the public to whom the dangers of radiation are still shrouded in mystery.

It is essential and appropriate that the benevolent uses of nuclear energy be the subject of discussion both by the experts and by laymen. The conference reported in this volume has taken this as its mission.

RICHARD F. HUMPHREYS,
President,
The Cooper Union
for the Advancement
of Science and Art

CONTENTS

Efrem A. Kahn

president and founder of E. A. Kahn & Co., Inc., electrical contractors and professional engineers, is the chairman of the Joint Industry Board of the Electrical Industry of New York. He heads the pension and welfare funds of the industry, as well as the scholarship committee and educational departments.

Mr. Kahn has been active for more than thirty years in trade association work. He is a former president of the New York Electrical Contractors' Association. He has been a member of many governmental committees for the study and improvement of city and state codes and standards, and for the improvement of practices. He was appointed by Governor Thomas E. Dewey to the committee to revise and standardize all building codes in the State of New York.

Harry Van Arsdale, Jr.

business manager of Local 3, International Brotherhood of Electrical Workers, is president of the New York City Central Labor Council, AFL-CIO, which represents one million workers in the metropolitan area.

Mr. Van Arsdale was initiated into Local 3 in 1925, and held various positions before becoming the union's business manager in 1934. He is known as a pioneer in establishing social benefits for union members, including interest-free loans for members buying homes, cars or cooperative apartments, and numerous educational benefits including scholarship programs at eight metropolitan colleges and universities. He is a trustee of Carnegie Hall and of the National Urban League, and is a director of the Lincoln Center for the Performing Arts.

THE NUCLEAR AGE CONFERENCE

In the winter of 1960, a group of leaders of the New York electrical industry visited with Professor Johnson E. Fairchild, Director of the Division of Adult Education of The Cooper Union. The appointment had been arranged for a discussion of the industry's relation to the imminent technological revolution occasioned by the arrival of the atomic age, nuclear age or whatever name was to be bestowed upon this new era in man's progress.

Since 1942, science had known that the radioactivity of uranium could be harnessed to produce heat continuously and under control. This became known as nuclear fission. The heat could be made to change water into steam, spin turbines, and thus generate electricity. This is what is meant by the phrase nuclear power.

The age of steam power began with Thomas Newcomen's invention and James Watt's improvements in the 18th century. But the impact of steam power was neither understood nor planned for; the Industrial Revolution just happened. It was quite obvious that whether the age of nuclear power meant liberation or destruction for mankind, the electrical industry would be quite involved.

[17

However, the social and industrial implications of this revolution were yet to be examined on a scholarly level.

The leaders of the electrical industry—both management and labor—wanted to find out what was happening and what would happen, so that as citizens they might understand and shape the impact of the Nuclear Age.

The Cooper Union was the logical place for this group to discuss such a problem. Since its establishment more than a century ago, the institution has interested itself in technology and art with a concurrent and equally deep concern with social philosophy. It was Peter Cooper's belief that technical education was insufficient to make the complete man.

Although he himself was a successful inventor, technician, and industrialist, Cooper believed in the broadest possible education. In the charter of the institution which he founded and endowed, and in the Deed of Trust in which he charged the trustees with their duties, he stressed the fundamental importance of—"social and political science, meaning thereby not merely the science of political economy, but the science and philosophy of a just and equitable form of government, based upon the great fundamental law that nations and men should do unto each other as they would be done by . . ." Indeed, the Division of Adult Education was formerly called the Division of Social Philosophy.

The New York electrical industry had already been working closely with Cooper Union's adult education division. Members of Local 3, International Brotherhood of Electrical Workers, had been taking Cooper Union courses for some time. David Landman, then assistant director of Cooper Union's adult education program, was assigned to plan a program that would bring some of the nation's best minds to explore with labor and industry leaders, the question:

When the era of plentiful nuclear power arrives, what will happen to the world, to America and to the electrical industry in particular?

For busy contractors, superintendents and foremen, a new adult-education technique was devised—a series of weekly breakfast meetings scheduled early enough so that a man could listen to a lecture, discuss problems of the future, and get away sufficiently early to deal with the problems of the present. Each session began with a man-sized breakfast at 8 A.M.; the meeting started promptly at 8:30 with an hour-long lecture; then questions, accompanied by an unceasing flow of coffee all the way through. Promptly at 10 o'clock the session ended. At The Cooper Union it was felt that the new format was advantageous since it permitted a turnout of industrialists and trade unionists who ordinarily would have found it difficult to assemble for five weekly meetings under any other time schedule.

Attendance, by invitation, averaged 95 men from the industry and Local 3 and, on occasion, other union leaders. Top-ranking engineering students from The Cooper Union were invited guests; other students sat at the back of the library of The Cooper Union where the meetings were held. The fifth and final session consisted of a field trip to Indian Point, site of the first nuclear power plant of the Consolidated Edison Company. Here practical men could see for themselves the translation of the abstract into reality.

One of the clichés of modern industrial life is the constant reiteration of pieties about labor and management meeting around the table to plan a golden future. Frequently these are the vaporings of something which goes by the pseudo-scientific name of public relations.

In our industry, we have kept to a minimum the creation of false images of labor-management relations of a nirvana-like character. We have worked together for more than 20 years with the full realization that the employer is an employer with his specific interests, and the worker is a worker with his. Where possible, without compromise of basic principles, we have sought to establish cooperative, friendly relations and an increased understanding of the problems of employers and workers.

That is why this program on the complications of a nuclear age that is already upon us was so resounding a success. It was a program adopting at the outset a pragmatic approach. Out of this program perhaps, may come a strengthening of the mutual understanding which has characterized the years of existence of the Joint Industry Board of the Electrical Industry. (This joint labor-management body administers the collective bargaining agreement in New York's electrical construction.)

This program is the first of the several to come. We have had a glimpse of the future, thanks to the scholars who gave us their time and effort. We know a little more now and, therefore, have some comprehension of how the electrical industry will be affected, in particular, and how society will be affected, in general. We have heard much to think about, and in the months ahead we plan to continue this expansion of the horizons of a key industry's members.

Above all, we have realized as never before how the very existence of freedom, now so threatened by totalitarian forces, can be strengthened not only in our own country, but in those new countries which today seek their place in the sun. Who knows—perhaps, this sun, whose warmth these disadvantaged countries live by, may in a few years become the very source from which an efficient form of power will be created to bring their day of genuine freedom nearer.

AMERICA FACES THE NUCLEAR AGE

Boris Pregel

the chairman of the board of trustees and past president
of the New York Academy of Sciences.

Dr. Pregel's studies and researches have ranged widely.
They include nucleonics, medical and industrial applications of radioactivity, the mechanics of phosphorescence,
and aerial exploration for radioactive mineral deposits. His
writings—published in France, Russia, Belgium and the
United States—include the significant monograph, *Peacetime Uses of Atomic Energy* (New York, 1947), a forerunner
of the present article.

THE IMPACT OF
THE NUCLEAR AGE

WHEN MAN first learned to use fire, he could
not guess at the effect this innovation would have on his
way of life. Neither could the men who developed the
wheel, the sail and the steam engine foresee more than
the most immediate effects of their inventions, yet they
vastly enriched human life and made irreversible modifications in society.

In this age, with history to inform us and greater technical and social knowledge to guide us, we ought to be more
sophisticated than our ancestors. We must be, for we are
in the act of taking the greatest leap forward in the history of mankind, one that will outdistance all those of the
past.

We have released the energy of the atom; we have entered the Nuclear Age. We cannot go back. We must therefore learn to control nuclear energy, well and safely, for
all men everywhere.

To gain an understanding of the problems of the Nuclear Age, we must first have a clear understanding of the
economic, political and social implications of Energy.

Energy is the basic tool of progress. No change, not even

the mitosis of a single cell, occurs without the spending of energy. Everything around us consists of what nature has provided, and of man's work, which is spent energy.

The citizen of ancient Rome had only a little bit more energy available to work for him than his primitive Etruscan ancestor; the Roman may have had a couple of slaves and a couple of horses. The citizen of medieval London had no more energy working for him than the Roman— and he did not live any better. But in the last 150 years, man has begun to harness the energy sources of his environment.

The first great changes came with the advent of the Industrial Age, based on engines that used energy stored in coal beds, which built cities and navies, wove textiles, and sent steam trains across the widest continents.

Since then, with energy from petroleum and the other sources, changes have come more swiftly. Today, radar telescopes scan the universe to record galactic explosions that occurred billions of years ago; oceanographic ships explore the undersea crust; electronic devices measure the earth's aura of unused energy and similar equipment traces inputs and outputs of single nerve cells; television cameras orbiting the earth send back photographs of entire subcontinents; electron microscopes photograph a virus; passenger planes fly at almost the speed of sound; and machines set type in Paris when a key is tapped in New York. These are only a few of the changes that our increasing supply of energy has made possible in the last 60 years.

In spite of the steamship and the railroad train and the Industrial Revolution, the world of 1900 more closely resembled that of 1660 than ours of 1960 in that it was a relatively stable world in which a few nations, most of them white, ruled great colonial areas. Although slavery had been abolished in the United States and most other areas, remnants of it and practices which resembled it still survived. The poor man and the man in the colonies "knew his place." He desired but did not yet demand adequate food and shelter. The habiliments of self-respect were beyond his reach. Today, all this is changed. It changed yesterday, in fact, and the sudden increase in the number of autonomous states is the outward, official, political evidence.

None of this could have come about without the expenditure of energy. The need for vastly greater supplies of it —to do vastly greater amounts of work and to satisfy not only our own increasing wants but those of the new nations—this is the central problem of the day. It would be an appalling problem except for the fact that nuclear energy makes it possible to meet those needs.

We must be spurred by the realization that the peoples of the countries recently become independent, or still to become so, are prepared to die to obtain their needs. These are dignity, independence, higher living standards—if one speaks as a social scientist. If one speaks as an engineer, the needs can be summed up in the phrase: adequate energy and its proper use. The magnitude of the problem is difficult to comprehend but we must try. The problem must be reduced because it grows as time passes, and because it is world-wide.

One way in which the problem grows is through the increase in man's numbers. World population is growing at an unprecedented rate: demographers predict that the 3 billion human beings on our planet today will increase to more than 5 billion by 1975, and to 7.5 billion by the year 2000. Since energy requirements are determined by two factors—the number of consumers and the needs of each consumer—it is evident that we must multiply today's available energy by almost three merely to satisfy the first factor. But to satisfy the second, that determined by the growth of each consumer's needs, we may have to double, quadruple, or decuple the supply of energy.

This raises the question: Where will this energy come from? Up to now, except for the 1½ per cent of our energy that has come from the hydroelectric installations, we have relied on coal, oil and gas. But these are raw materials as well as fuels, and when depleted, they are irreplaceable. It is irrational to continue to use them for production of energy if better sources are available. Moreover, there is a special politico-economic hazard in reliance on oil, for oil fields are not uniformly distributed throughout the world, and oil-producing countries are vulnerable to such political and military crises as we have witnessed in recent years in the Middle East, North Africa, and Venezuela. More hydroelectric power is not the answer to the energy question, either, even if water power plants are erected on every suitable site. By 1980, we shall simply be unable to meet the needs by using conventional sources of power. We shall have to make use of either nuclear energy, solar energy, the tides or the winds. Although research is going on in all these fields, the only new form in which technology is sufficiently advanced is nuclear energy.

Nuclear energy has advantages as a power source for both advanced and backward regions:

It can function anywhere. It is independent of geography, climate and the general cultural level of the inhabitants.

Upkeep is minimal. It does not require supplies of water, coal or oil. Needed amounts of nuclear fuel are easily transported, and the consumed weight is negligible.

Operation is automatic and can be managed by a limited personnel.

And because initial costs are high (and nuclear fuels are and will remain government property), installations will continue to be planned and financed by national or multi-national agencies. They can therefore be placed where they are needed.

The United States is less in need of the new energy sources than the rest of the world. At the first conference on Peacetime Uses of Atomic Energy, held in 1955 at Geneva, it was reported that world production of electric energy was approximately 1500 billion kilowatt hours, of which 625 billion—40 per cent—was produced and used in the United States. Western Europe and the Soviet Union were poor in comparison, but they were rich in contrast with the truly poor countries in other parts of the world, particularly those which are now emerging from colonial status. Many of the latter have populations that are increasing rapidly; most have almost no native fuels. A generation or two ago, moderate improvements in their agriculture or industry would have meant prosperity, progress and peaceful evolution. Today the production of mouths outruns the benefits gained from irrigation and new hydropower installations. These countries need massive increases in their energy supply.

The Geneva Conference set 6,000 billion kilowatt hours as the probable world production of electric power in 1975 —four times what was produced in 1955. Even if this much power could be produced in conventional plants, it could not be transported to where it was needed. History shows that the hungry and wronged attempt to better their conditions by violence, but that prosperous and happy men effect what may be truly revolutionary changes by peaceful means. Nuclear reactors promise peaceful aggrandizement to the have-not nations of the world.

It may be useful to point out here that the endowments

of peoples we choose to call "advanced" or "industrially competent" or "cultured" differ from those of men in the most "backward" regions chiefly in one respect: the "advanced" man has had energy to spare, and the "backward" man has not. Otherwise men are, so far as scientific tests can show, a single species with apparently uniform potential. The difference between a polished, erudite African and a savage of the jungle may be only twenty years or less of schooling. In most parts of the world, therefore, the engineers and technicians required to operate reactors and distribute power can be provided in a relatively few years. Within two generations, populations can become able to provide not only reactor operators, but also factory managers and specialists in the distribution of goods. In fact, within this period every have-not nation in the world can become a land of plenty. Where literacy and other circumstances permit, the change can come even more swiftly.

Indeed, such a revolution should create less confusion among backward peoples than the corresponding changes cause among the most advanced. This paradox is already observable in many parts of the world today where the airplane is supplanting the bullock cart or dogsled, where the radio directly supercedes the village drum for communications, and where manufacturing goes from handicraft all the way to automation without having to pass through the states symbolized by the steam railway and assembly line. The peoples who make these swift changes will never face the stern necessity which the industrialized nations now face—of having to rebuild their capital structure and retrain millions of workers whose usefulness has been obliterated by automation.

Let us consider a fictional, energy-deficient undeveloped nation. Call it Nation A.

Nation A has neither coal nor oil. It has a seaport, but no railways. Trucks and buses carry produce and passengers from inland areas to the seaport, which is also its capital. Paths suitable for bicycles and footpaths connect the smaller outlying villages with each other and with the highways.

Nation A's major crop is one which grows wild or requires a minimum of cultivation and processing before it is shipped for sale.

Schools were established in the seaport three generations ago by missionaries with support from colonial authority. Two generations ago such schools were established in the larger inland villages. Then, schools were set up in many of the more remote jungle villages with teachers drawn from among graduates of the mission schools. In the last decade several schools have been upgraded to college-preparatory level. The elite of the nation are graduates of these high schools and of colleges in the homeland of the former colonial authority. Most of them hold degrees in law, literature and political science, but there are a few physicians, physicists, botanists, biologists and chemists. Altogether, these constitute barely one per cent of the total population. Eighty per cent of the people are entirely illiterate and about ten per cent have no better than a fourth-grade education. Only half of the remainder have entered high school.

The greatest needs of Nation A are:

An adequate and balanced diet for all its people.
An effective public-health program.
Education for all—in the next generation at least to the
    eighth-grade level.
Weatherproof housing.
Adequate clothing.
Newspapers, magazines, radio, television.

All-weather highways and sufficient conveyances for public use.

Power, especially electrical power.

The last need, of course, is the critical one. It probably cannot be utilized to full advantage until the other needs are met at least in part, but neither can its partial satisfaction wait.

Let us assume, therefore, that Nation A gets its first reactor within five years, and that it is located in the capital city where, because of the existence of a conventional power plant and some light industry, a promising nucleus of technically trained and trainable persons already exists. This working force, under imported engineers and technicians, will man a factory for the processing of the nation's primary market crop, and will lay out, build and maintain the power lines which carry electricity to the surrounding countryside. On the periphery, the chief uses of this energy, initially, will be to provide light, water supply, sanitary facilities, and air conditioning for public buildings (schools, central assembly places, refrigeration plants and laundries), and for stoves, lights, water and air conditioning in homes.

The second reactor in Nation A should probably be installed in the far interior; or the second step may be reactors for areas with previously established concentrations of population or potentially valuable crops or ores. These steps would set up a chain reaction: the educational program required to train workers to man the first reactor and factory would provide the faculties, and the incentive, for the creation of more and more schools to keep ahead of the uses for power that would continually be opening up.

The pattern of development and enrichment sketched for Nation A can be repeated in all the world's undeveloped lands. Nuclear energy is the answer to the have-not nations' needs. It can function as well in Tibet, High Peru or Greenland, in the Matto Grosso of Brazil or the steaming jungles of Ghana. Furthermore, the establishment of nuclear power installations where and when they are needed will correct the gravest flaw in today's world economy, the flaw largely responsible for the rancor exhibited by so many emergent nations. The fact is that the advanced western nations have exported their most valuable cultural asset—education—without being able or foresighted enough to export energy or enough of what energy will buy: food, health, clothing and housing. Education has made the have-nots conscious of what they do not have.

The turmoil of the new nations and the spiritual distress of the West can be attributed to our failure to develop social techniques as advanced as our scientific techniques. Distribution of wealth is essentially a social technique, and it is time we undertook to master it. In technology, we have moved into the twenty-first century; we can no longer afford to cling to nineteenth-century thinking. This is the problem for statesmen, economists, sociologists. It is not a problem for the leaders of any one or two nations, powerful though those nations might be. It must be studied and governed by an organization of all the nations. This could well be in the framework of the existing world organization, the United Nations, whether in its present form or reorganized.

World-wide availability of nuclear energy will make necessary not only world-wide distribution but a world plan for production. If some countries, like the United States, can produce steel more advantageously than others, why should Japan or India build steel mills? Perhaps India should concentrate on fibers, Canada on cellulose, Argentina on beef. Why should England allocate any of its limited acres to raising meat animals, or Egypt undertake to produce aluminum? The world of abundance will be, inescapably, one world.

In Europe and in the United States, as in the have-not nations, reactors will be a monopoly of government. In a conventional power installation, the initial investment covers construction and machinery; fuels are purchased as needed. But in a nuclear installation, the initial investment must cover fuel as well as construction and machinery, for a nuclear reactor has to be fully loaded to function. Two reasons, therefore, compel governments to finance nuclear power plants: the fuel is very costly, and it is a potential weapon.

There are other reasons. In the present stage of knowledge, a great deal of research remains to be done: many types of reactors must be constructed and tested to discover which is most efficient. Sufficient private capital cannot be found to meet the sheer magnitude of capital requirement of this absolutely essential research. Moreover, from personal experience, I know that private capital will go only where there is promise of a return in the foreseeable future, and it is difficult to predict when nuclear power will be profitable. It requires no great prescience to know that the reactors being built now will be outmoded by newer ones which may be three or four or twenty times as efficient. We cannot expect private capital to build, pay for, and then scrap the fantastically costly early models, and, indeed, it is not doing so. If we examine the circumstances under which "privately owned" reactors are being *built and fueled,* we shall discover that the major investor is government. Plants like Indian Point, Yankee and Elk River, while constructed with private capital, are fueled with the aid of a generous subsidy that is embodied in fuel-enrichment using the power of the T.V.A., in a fuel-use charge deliberately set below cost, and in the waiving of the fuel-use charge during the first year or two of the reactor's operation. Power reactors today are not, except in name, examples of private capital.

I shall return to this question of government ownership later, in an examination of what nuclear power can mean to the United States, but this seems a suitable point at which to discuss the general question of the cost.

A widely-accepted fallacy is that nuclear power will inevitably cost too much to compete with conventionally-generated power. One cannot argue that the cost of atomic power *today* is competitive (except in countries or regions where conventional-fuel installations produce energy only at excessively high cost). But if we remember that today's most advanced reactor can be compared in efficiency with an automobile of 1900, it is obvious that anything so crude is certain to be tremendously improved. In Britain, in 1960, scientists and engineers predicted that reactors then under construction would produce energy for half the cost of existing models, while with foreseeable improvements, subsequent models would produce energy for one quarter the cost. In America, in 1961, a responsible engineer said that a nuclear plant could be completed in four years which would produce power cheaper than perhaps half the country's present coal- or oil-burning plants.*

Scientists and engineers generally concede there is no insoluble problem that will prevent eventual production of power at no cost at all. The breeder reactor promises just that. It is a development so out of line with our habit of thinking in terms of scarcity that it is difficult to grasp. This is the principle: the breeder reactor employs uranium

---

* Dr. Robert B. Richards of General Electric Co., speaking before the American Power Conference in Chicago, March, 1961. He forecast nuclear power at 6.56 mills per kilowatt-hour, decreasing to 6.0 mills.

(U-235) for the production of neutrons to convert stable uranium (U-238) into the element plutonium (Pu-239). The relative proportions of U-235 and U-238 and the superiority of Pu-239 over U-235 as fuel, promise an increase in power output on the order of 100 to 1.

Uranium ore, the fuel for present nuclear power plants, is not in short supply. Recent exploration has shown that uranium is a common mineral not just in North America and the Congo but in many regions. And the world is not likely to run short of nuclear-energy material for another reason: in the long run, atomic fusion is more promising as a source of energy than atomic fission, and the oceans contain immeasurable quantities of tritium (H-3), which is the known raw material for fusion. Moreover, the tritium in sea water appears to be constantly being replenished. The problem of harnessing the fusion reaction for peaceful purposes is certain to be solved and certain to relieve the demand for uranium—although we can expect that the fission process will probably continue to be used.

Let us examine the coming impact of nuclear energy on the United States, which is the archetype of the industrialized nations of the West. It has been said that civilization began with the creation of the city, an event as influential as the invention of the steam engine. Urbanization brought men together in an organized way; it provided for specialization of effort and for the sharing of the benefits—streets, waterworks, irrigation systems, law courts, taxation, temples, arts and records—the pooled wealth of the inhabitants and their progenitors. The cities of the prehistoric era were supported chiefly by agriculture; those of the ancient Mediterranean and medieval worlds appear to have added plunder and trade as sources of wealth. In the Industrial Age, the demands of manufacturing, communication and transport produced the great urban complexes of New York and nearby seaport cities, of Detroit and Chicago (as well as the Ruhr, London, and the others). Here great clots of humanity were held close to the forge and lathe and loom, in locations where water and rails were available to carry all over the world the goods men made. But the factors which determined the location and growth of these centers are no longer decisive; there no longer remains a reason for these massive social thrombi. The atrophy of the cities is under way.

Nuclear energy will speed dispersion of large-city populations, but a greater stimulus will come from automation. The latter development while not caused by the introduction of atomic energy, has been promoted by it and comes concurrently. Automated installations are such lavish users of electrical energy that they can be operated only where the power supply is cheap and abundant. Automation is therefore the junior partner to nuclear power.

Automation will wipe out whole strata of labor including that part of the industrial labor force performing repetitive or limited-judgment tasks. The trend is irreversible. It will affect most directly the specialized skilled and semiskilled workers who, within a few decades, will be relegated to the ranks of unskilled labor. Machines will take over the work of men's hands and minds; increasingly we shall see fewer workers on the production lines. Soon our industrial plants will resemble electric power-plants, with automatic machines arranged in functional patterns and a few supervisors to check dials and lights. Electronic devices are already replacing humans in banks, insurance firms, and in other commercial establishments that require extensive calculations. For, while in all history before 1945, devices increased man's ability to calculate by about a hundred times, since 1945 the electronic computers have increased the speed of calculation by a factor of 250 thousand.* A similar displacement of manpower is going on in research and development, in chemical plants, in road building and other construction.

Although automation is only in its infancy, we are already witnessing the phenomenon of obsolescence: the massive machines employing vacuum tubes are being replaced by smaller, less expensive devices using transistors. At the same time, machines are being developed which will take over the human function of supervising machines and correcting mistakes. It appears quite certain that machines will soon be made which can, under certain conditions, exercise better-than-human judgment; and machines that can think, learn, grow and make duplicates of themselves with built-in instructions to do useful work. This process can continue indefinitely.

The inevitable growth of automation, more than anything else, will make the great city obsolete. In the New York metropolitan area alone, hundreds of thousands of white collar, skilled and semiskilled workers will lose their jobs. In other urban areas like Detroit, where the emphasis is even greater on hard goods, the number of the technologically unemployed will be greater.

These prospects make job-retraining on a nationwide scale a prime imperative, else the millions who will otherwise be incapable of productive labor will become a threat to the rest of the country. They will be susceptible to the incitements of demagogues who will seek to use them to gain political power. The greater the concentration of these automation-age displaced persons, the greater the threat to a stable social order. For this reason alone, I sug-

---

* *Electronic Industries,* January, 1961.

gest that the dispersion of our great accumulations of urban population will be necessary.

As a further consequence of unemployment and the threat it poses, I foresee:

Increase in adult education programs;
Multiplication of persons employed in service jobs;
Reduction of the normal working week by half or more.

The proliferation of educational programs for adults is certain to continue and to expand. As workers are displaced by automation, classes will no longer be restricted to night hours. They will fill every available classroom and require very competent teachers in order to equip men and women for lives that will be new in the type of occupation and in the amount and quality of the leisure with which they will be overladen. This is a problem which demands serious study by our educational authorities.

What sort of retraining program, for example, should be set up for X hundred thousand bookkeepers aged 35 to 50? And should any attempt be made at all to retrain those over 50? Some of the answers will have to come from Industry itself which has recently shown a willingness to undertake some of the responsibility for postgraduate education of its scientific and engineering personnel. But reeducation for new jobs is only part of what is sorely needed. The massive requirement is for training in the socially desirable use of leisure.

Because man's culture has until now been conditioned by scarcity, we have valued money above music, industriousness above art, and material possessions above beauty or morality or pleasure. It could not have been otherwise. As an unhappy consequence, however, we now find that our resources of leisure-time activities are solely insufficient. Television and bowling are unlikely to provide satisfactions sufficient to fill the empty hours by which we are about to be overwhelmed. To any except those who choose not to see, it is clear that our society, at all levels, must undertake to educate people to use free time constructively. Moreover, we must act immediately. It will not be easy to re-educate our masses in one generation or one lifetime, but I fear this is all the time we have.

So far we have considered only the impact of nuclear energy on manufacturing and the commerce associated with it. We must not overlook the fact that agriculture also will be affected. After machinery made it possible to substitute the energy of draft animals for human effort in reaping and threshing, then steam power supplanted the animals. In the last two generations, internal combustion engines have replaced the horse in the field and electricity has taken over human labor in the barn and farmyard, making it possible often for one man to do work that formerly required five men. A century ago, 85 per cent of our population lived on the land. Today only 12 per cent of us live on the land; nevertheless we pile up mountainous surpluses of food. During the hundred years that have seen this change in farm manpower, new advances in biology have given us more viable and more productive plants and animals. The cultivation of algae, now in the research stage, promises practically unlimited food supplies for the future. Nuclear energy is playing its part also, producing deliberate mutations in food plants that will further increase production. The future's food supplies, looked at in this light, are so well-assured that they should put a stop to philosophizing about the need to limit human reproduction.

How can we use nuclear power to solve the *real* over-population problem—too many persons without jobs and too many without inner resources to use and enjoy their leisure? By using both nuclear power and automation to disperse the population and to pay the cost of improving our society.

The first can be accomplished without coercion by making it possible for the technologically unemployed of our cities to obtain new jobs elsewhere, chiefly in what we may call "expanded service industries." A simple and direct way in which this can be done, is for the federal government to begin a program of building nuclear reactors away from the large centers of population. Power produced by these reactors should be offered to industries at attractive rates for use in automated plants that would employ retrained workers from the cities. In turn, the homes and families of these production workers will create employment for tradesmen and teachers, plumbers and preachers, doctors, dentists, musicians, milkmen and social workers—all the services the production workers could afford.

The reactor-centered communities may either be self-sufficient or one-product, one-activity groupings. The important element is that the communities be homogeneous, prosperous, relatively small and, as a consequence, relatively stable. The production workers of these communities will in the beginning be retrained specialists from semi-automatic industry. Those in service jobs may or may not be retrained, since professional and trade skills will carry over. There will be a great, and probably growing, need for artists and entertainers; the short work week will create strong demands for leisure-time opportunities such as only large cities offer today. The writing of sonatas and sonnets and plays, the creation of paintings and sculpture, the study of literature, philosophy and the dance and games—all these higher expressions of man's humanity serve the needs of the soul, needs which increase as our physical needs are gratified.

I have suggested the dispersal of dangerous accumulations of unemployed persons as an engineering approach to a sociological problem. Building reactors, I have said, is a clear responsibility of the federal government. Using the experimental reactors to create new jobs and cities where jobs and populations do not now exist, is to go one step further. In the long run, when, with research problems solved, nuclear power produces more wealth than it costs, we can expect it to return the investment many times over, and for as long as we care to peer into the future. Since the government will own all nuclear plants and since they will have become almost the sole source of industrial power, I suggest that the government will be able to sell or rent energy at a rate that can replace taxation.

It is interesting to speculate about this. Suppose taxation as we now know it were eliminated and a nuclear fuel rent substituted. If such rents were the only source of federal-government income, tax bookkeeping and related problems of both government and industry would be vastly simplified, and most individuals would go scot-free. Such a single tax, imposed at the source, would have many virtues. Its simplicity makes it appealing to a population which, after more than 40 years, has still not mastered the intricacies of the income tax form nor acquired the discipline needed for keeping accurate accounts. One may hope that this simplicity would appeal also to a treasury department which has apparently been as confused as the citizen by the tax laws and its own regulations.

The nuclear-fuel-rent tax could be instituted in the reactor-centered communities first, by making the payments a deductible expense against income. As nuclear power became cheaper and cheaper to produce, the rent paid to the government would eventually exceed its cost.

Meanwhile, the government could enhance the advantages of the new communities so as to encourage relocation of factories in them, and so speed the day when nuclear rents supported the government. As nuclear energy became the major power source, the government would undoubtedly see the necessity of assuming ownership of the other major energy sources, the hydroelectric and conventional thermal plants. (The latter might be abolished completely, and coal and petroleum used exclusively as chemical raw materials.)

Industries essential to the public welfare—food and textile processing plants, for example—would pay low fuel-rent taxes, whereas the cost of fuel would be graduated upward until luxury goods industries paid the highest rate of all. Schools, museums, public halls and the properties of non-profit institutions would pay little tax or none. State taxes could very well disappear, with Congress providing what share of the federal revenue the states needed. Local town and city taxes—for sewers and sidewalks, schools and constables—might continue indefinitely.

If we keep in mind that energy is the basic tool of life and that all we regard as wealth is no more than spent energy, or the symbol of spent energy, this idea of taxing energy and nothing more is probably less revolutionary than the idea of taxing *profits* seemed when it was first proposed.

I wish to emphasize that throughout this discussion of the impact of nuclear energy on the peoples of the world, I have written only as an engineer. I have stated as fact that which I accept as fact and as opinions or speculations that which is in the nature of prediction. Of those predictions which are based on engineering data, I can say that I consider them sound, and I repeat them:

We shall have cheap nuclear energy.

It will remain a government monopoly.

We shall build reactors in out-of-the-way places.

If we build them for the use of manufacturers, then new cities will grow up around them, setting a new pattern for urban living.

Between nuclear energy and automation, the standard of living will rise for the employed, creating a need for more education for the employed, and a need for re-education for the technologically *un*employed.

To this list of predictions, I should like to append a short sermon: Any attempt by entrenched beneficiaries of the status quo to stem the changes—whether by men of capital or management or labor or government—is bound to fail. History teaches that attempts to stop technological progress have never succeeded. No victories were won; only delaying actions. To oppose new trends too strenuously may be fatal to those who try to resist; in fact, such resistance could ruin both industry and workers and even the state.

I have no illusions about the magnitude of the problems we face or the difficulty of finding solutions. I know well that the solutions will not come of themselves.

Along with an understanding of the promise the future holds, the world's peoples must be strengthened or protected against the trials that are certain to accompany our changeover from an economy of scarcity to one of abundance. Small wars, insurrections, what I have termed wars of dispossession, may occur; if they do they will delay the time when all will share abundance. The task of enlightened men must be to appease the hunger and slake the thirst of the impoverished majority of men in such ways that cataclysm is averted and peace may abide, with abundance everywhere among all men.

John Ray Dunning

a nuclear physicist, has served on the faculty at Columbia University since 1929 and has been Dean of the Faculty of Engineering and Applied Science since 1950.

Dr. Dunning was the first scientist to measure the energy released from nuclear fission, and the first man to demonstrate nuclear fission in this country. As a leading figure in the Manhattan Project, he designed the gaseous diffusion process plant for the separation of uranium isotopes at Oak Ridge, which became the basis for America's military and peacetime nuclear energy programs.

Dr. Dunning is at present a scientific advisor to the Defense Department and the various services, and consultant to many other government agencies. He is one of the leaders in the program for the orderly development of nuclear power in New York State.

CHAPTER TWO

THE WHAT AND HOW
OF NUCLEAR POWER

IT IS NOW over twenty years since the discovery of
atomic fission. Because the world first learned of nuclear
energy through the explosion of the bombs over Hiroshima
and Nagasaki, terrible catastrophes have been predicted.
There have also been predictions of Utopia, with energy
so cheap that it would not even be metered, and with all
our industries and societies remade overnight. Obviously,
neither utopia nor world destruction has proved inevitable, but nuclear energy *has* begun to come out of the
laboratories as the great source of energy for the decades
ahead.

A vast amount of public information and technical
exposition has been circulated in the past ten years. We
have developed ways of presenting the physics—and some
of the engineering—of fission and fusion, so that nuclear
phenomena are no longer the sinister mysteries they were
back in the 1940's. In those days the words "chain reaction" were almost like a witch's curse to a considerable
portion of the population. I am afraid we still have some
way to go in public education concerning the actual
realities of the atomic age.

Now, I do not want to go deeply into the scientific aspects of atomic energy. I want rather to discuss current technology, and to suggest what engineers and scientists see ahead in the age of nuclear power. Although we talk in a theoretical way about fusion and about devices for converting nuclear energy directly into electricity, the fact remains that, for the foreseeable future, atomic energy technology will be based on the use of uranium as a prime fuel material. Uranium is one of the less common elements, but not nearly as uncommon as many people thought. There is enough uranium in the world to serve as the major source of energy to light homes and run factories for at least a century ahead, and very likely two centuries—far more energy than there is in our usual fossil fuels, coal, oil and natural gas. Those are really degraded nuclear energy—past energies of nuclear origin that flowed to us from the sun and were chemically stored. In turning to atomic energy, we are turning to the primary source of energy in the universe, instead of using a long indirect cycle.

Uranium as found in nature is, like most elements, a mixture of atoms that are chemically alike but of slightly different weights. Ordinary uranium is 99.3 per cent U-238 and about 0.7 per cent U-235.* The rarer, lighter variety, uranium-235, is the starting point of all atomic fission processes that we know today, because it is the only fissionable material found in nature. We isolate uranium-235; we separate it from bulk uranium in huge, complex plants in Oak Ridge, Tennessee; Paducah, Kentucky; and Portsmouth, Ohio. This is done by the gaseous diffusion process, which makes use of the principle that if a mixture of gases of different weights is pumped through a porous

---

* The number 235 refers to the atom's mass, which is 235 times the mass of an atom of hydrogen, the lightest element.

membrane, the lighter atoms will pass through slightly more rapidly; thus the gas mixture at the far side of the membrane will have an increased percentage of the lighter gas. At Oak Ridge, uranium is combined with flourine to make uranium hexafluoride gas, which is pumped through membranes, again and again, until the material has a high proportion of the useful U-235 atoms. Nearly ten per cent of the total electric power in the United States has been used for separating uranium-235. Most of this unfortunately has been going into atomic weapons, but it is equally usable for peaceful purposes.

In addition to U-235, we have two other kinds of "synthetic" atomic fuels which we can make in the huge atomic reactors. One was first developed on a large scale at Hanford, Washington. Through a chain reaction based on uranium-235, we bombarded ordinary uranium-238 with neutrons, converting it to plutonium-239, a fissionable material roughly as useful as uranium-235. Through a similar process, we can convert another element, thorium, into an artificially-produced isotope of uranium, U-233. These three atomic fuels, the one found in nature and the two man-made ones, are the base fuels of the present atomic age. Actually, since plutonium and uranium-233 are secondary derived fuels, they will not be major factors in nuclear power for a number of decades.

Now, how do we use the nuclear fuels? A one-inch cube of uranium-235, which weighs about a pound, contains the energy equivalent to about four million pounds of coal. At present, it is concentrated by the Atomic Energy Commission and sold—or more accurately, leased—to our power companies. It is sold or given abroad to our allies for research and for power purposes through various kinds of bilateral treaties. The price depends on how pure in U-235 the material is. If it is about 90 per cent uranium-235, the

price is in the neighborhood of $8,000 a pound. In air-
plane and submarine power plants, we generally use
uranium with a high proportion of U-235. In public utilities power plants, the reactors are usually designed for a
uranium mixture with two, three or four times the natural
concentration of U-235, that is, one and a half per cent to
three per cent instead of the 0.7 per cent which is normal
in nature. This uranium is fabricated into metal rods or
flat sheets. Or, for our more advanced reactors, we use not
the pure metal but uranium oxide, UO_2, stamped into
pellets and placed in stainless steel or Zircaloy tubes.

In the future, we shall probably use more exotic uranium compounds such as uranium carbide, which stands
high temperatures very well—it goes up to 5000 degrees
without melting or becoming deformed. With such temperatures we can begin to achieve atomic power's full potential. There are no reactors running with uranium carbide
so far, but there is talk of refueling some of the newer
reactors (like the Consumers' Public Power reactor in
Nebraska) with it.

The heart of any reactor is simply a sufficient amount of
nuclear fuel to maintain the desired, heat-producing chain
reaction. With pure U-235, the critical amount is generally
at least several pounds; a typical fuel loading of a big
reactor might be twenty tons of uranium containing two
per cent of uranium-235. This amount of uranium is
formed into half-inch-diameter rods and immersed in what
is called a moderator, whose function is to slow down the
neutrons which bombard the atomic nuclei and split them,
releasing more neutrons which split more nuclei, and so
on, in a self-sustaining chain reaction. Frequently, present-
day reactors use water as a moderator; but carbon in
graphite form was the first moderator and is still used. We
have had chain reactions going since about 1942. In the

first really big reactors at Hanford, Washington, all the heat was thrown away into the Columbia River, for we were not interested in heat then; we wanted only to make plutonium. We began reversing this ghastly waste of energy in the early fifties.

The first big power reactor in this country was the Shippingport Reactor of Duquesne Light and Power Company, near Pittsburgh. Here Westinghouse used what was essentially the reactor design developed for the Navy for use in the submarine *Nautilus*. This has actually been rather expensive, as one would expect on the first round; but it has had a very good operating record and has shown marked economies in its second re-fueling.

Atomic fuels, of course, have a limited lifetime. The one-pound chunk of uranium we talked of—the equal of four million pounds of coal—sounds like a lot, but a typical city power plant is likely to burn that much coal in one day. In time, nuclear fuel is "burned" into fission products, and eventually the chain reaction slows down and stops. We rate the efficiency of a reactor in megawatt days per ton of material. Formerly, we got perhaps a thousand megawatt days per ton; fuel did not last very long. Today's reactors may run as high as 15,000 megawatt days per ton, and we expect that this figure will be increased. We are getting to where we can expect a nuclear plant to run almost two years or more at full power on the first loading of fuel.

Safety is another point which has great economic importance. Speaking frankly as an engineer, I can say that we have all leaned so far backward that we have enormously increased the cost of nuclear power plants. To make reactors very safe, we put them in containment vessels, those typical round domes you see in pictures. For a while, the reactor dome is going to be a familiar feature on the

American landscape, but I hope we will get over that phase. We already have designs for containment under ground, using water suppression, and there are other schools of thought. But, certainly for the next ten years, atomic power plants will be characterized by those spherical containment shells, which are obviously expensive.

The use of a reactor in a power station is simple: it heats water, just as a coal-fired boiler does in a conventional power plant; it produces steam to drive turbines. There is scientific speculation about devices that will convert radiation energy directly into electrical energy, but a long, long time will be needed before these will supplant the reactors and conventional generators.

There are several major varieties of nuclear-reactor power plants, and an enormous number of subspecies. The simplest is the so-called "boiling water" reactor, with direct-cycle natural circulation. The reactor vessel with its tubular uranium fuel elements is immersed in water; steam is produced, rises into the bell at the top and goes directly to a steam turbine which turns the generator and generates electricity; the condensed water is taken back to the reactor vessel to be heated again. This is the simplest atomic power plant. Commonwealth Edison Company in Chicago has placed in operation a plant of this type.

A variation of this, the so-called "pressurized water" type, was developed first because engineers were not sure that the simpler version would work. In this setup, the water under high pressure picks up heat in the reactor and goes to the heat exchangers of an intermediate steam generator; there is no direct contact between the water of the reactor and the steam that goes into the turbine. This is the design used in the *Nautilus* and Shippingport; it is basically the design used in Indian Point by Consolidated Edison.

With present technology, these reactors generate steam of only 1000 degrees—and more realistically, 700 or 800 degrees F. Conventional fuels bring steam, by superheating, up to 1200 or even 1400 degrees; the turbine-generator to which the steam is then fed can therefore be more efficient. Since atomic power-plant technology is still unable to match these temperatures, one solution is to use a reactor to generate steam at perhaps 800 degrees, then to run the steam through an oil- or gas-fired superheater. Such superheaters are incorporated today in only one or two plants, of which Indian Point is the first. To a nuclear purist, it might seem wrong to put an oil-fired job on top of a reactor—it's against the club rules—but we may have more of such combinations because they are sound engineering. However, engineers are studying ways of superheating steam in reactors so as to be able to use nuclear power all the way.

I have been serving recently as chairman of the Empire State Utility Power Resources group, and, as part of our studies toward the building of the next nuclear power plant in New York State, we have been reviewing the presentations of all the manufacturers of nuclear plants. Generally, the power plants are good-sized ones—300 megawatts and larger—and are priced in the $60 million to $85 million range. Atomic power was originally rather expensive, and to some degree it still is, for we are still in a stage of rapid research and development. As one increases the size of a power plant from 100 to 200, 300, and 500 megawatts, the cost in mills per kilowatt-hour comes down. This is true, of course, whether one uses atomic power or coal, oil or gas: the bigger the plant, the cheaper the unit cost. When one gets above 200 or 300 megawatts, one approaches costs of 7 to 8 mills per kilowatt-hour. This is getting electricity generated by nuclear power down into the cost range of conventional power plants in areas that are distant from coal mines.

Power costs for a 330 megawatt closed-cycle plant work out approximately this way: About 3.3 mills of the cost is capital investment; about $\frac{1}{2}$ mill represents land; about 3 mills represents the atomic fuel; and about $\frac{1}{2}$ mill goes for operation and maintenance. This is a rough but fair representation of the kind of cost figures one finds today. I think they may be a little optimistic.

The future of atomic power rests on a fact that I have been trying to explain to many people for many years: the steeply rising costs of fossil fuels—coal, oil and gas. In the New York City area, energy costs are approaching 40¢ per billion B.T.U. In New England, we figure 50¢. In Europe we figure 75¢ or $1.00. Here, then, is the basic point: the choice between an atomic plant and a fossil-fuel plant depends on the location of the plant and the shipping costs of the fossil fuels. Power cost rises almost as a straight line plotted against the cost of coal, oil or gas. A nuclear plant, however, is a flat curve. (A recent study shows that nuclear costs could actually come down somewhat. There are those who think that uranium fuel costs should be about two-thirds of the price the government is presently charging industry.) The real point is that the trend of fossil fuel costs is bound to be upward in the long run, while nuclear power plants will for the foreseeable future tend to get cheaper.

Coal and oil costs are steadily rising for a variety of reasons. Natural gas is going higher all the time; we are having to reach further for our natural gas, piping it in from Canada and Mexico. Nuclear fuel costs are likely to go down, and the efficiency of utilization of nuclear fuel is also improving. Nuclear plants are likewise coming down in capital costs. Further, a fueling, instead of lasting a few weeks, now lasts about a year; soon, a fueling should last several years. By taking advantage of research and improvements in technology, nuclear power plants are increasingly competing in the fossil-fuel markets.

Around 1910, we paid about 15 mills per kilowatt-hour in fuel and plant costs to generate electricity using fossil fuels. These costs steadily decreased until around 1950, when improved technology began to lose the battle with inflation in coal and labor costs. From 1961 to 1975, the cost of power generated by fossil fuels will inevitably increase.

On the other hand, the costs of generating electricity by nuclear fuel, which started very high in the middle 1950's —20 mills, much higher than fossil fuel—have been coming down steeply. Most engineers think the cost-curves will cross in the 1960's; I do not believe anybody today thinks it will be as late as the 1970's. Yet, I personally doubt that we will ever generate electricity more cheaply in a nuclear-powered plant than in a fossil-fuel plant right on top of a coal mine in West Virginia, or right on top of a gas well in Texas.

Nuclear technology, therefore, has progressed from a scientific curiosity to an expensive device that is uniquely useful for such purposes as powering the *Nautilus,* to a practical commercial possibility. We are seeing, right now, the dawn of actual, economic atomic power.

Nuclear power plants are now being sold on a firm-priced basis. One still has to be careful about extras such as site costs, but the manufacturers will guarantee a fixed price; they will guarantee fuel costs; they will guarantee fuel life. And when they guarantee 15,000 megawatt days, this is probably a conservative estimate—otherwise they would not give guarantees.

We still do have a problem in re-fueling and waste disposal. Under the new program of the State Office of Atomic Development that the legislature is implementing, New York State itself will cooperate in a waste disposal system. Actually, the problem is not much worse than the problem of disposal of garbage in New York City, if one looks at it carefully and without fright. We shall also need in New York State a central re-fueling, reprocessing plant (which ought to be right next to the disposal area) for re-working the spent atomic fuel. The reduced residue can then be buried, perhaps in an abandoned salt mine, so that it will not trouble anyone. There are a number of suitable interesting sites, possibly on the Hudson River where atomic ships would go up for re-fueling. One does have to handle the fuel elements with proper lead protection and so on, but that technique is being mastered.

We have here, in short, an established, growing business. Not all the American electrical equipment manufacturers would be quite optimistic, of course, as they have all taken something of a beating during the early phase of the atomic business. But business is improving. In the next three or four years, I predict that the importance of nuclear power in our United States economy will be established as the result of technical advances. The pioneers are out in the field designing, not utopia, but a cheaper and more abundant source of energy to power man's aspirations for a better life.

Gordon R. Milne

assistant vice president since 1959 for Consolidated Edison Company of New York, Inc., is a graduate of Stevens Institute of Technology. He served in a variety of engineering positions in the company prior to his appointment as chief mechanical engineer in 1958.

For many years, Mr. Milne has been responsible for the mechanical design and over-all efficiency of the company's generating plants. He has played a leading role in conceiving and designing Con Edison's Indian Point atomic plant which is nearing completion at Buchanan, New York, and has addressed professional organizations in this country and abroad on the application of nuclear energy to the generation of electric power.

CHAPTER THREE

INDIAN POINT: A CASE STUDY

NUCLEAR POWER will come to New York when Con Edison's hundred million dollar Indian Point nuclear electric generating station begins its operational tests early in 1962. Nuclear power will then join the alternating-current network, the pulverized fuel, water-wall boiler, high-voltage underground transmission and other major advances in the art of generating and distributing electric power to which Con Edison has made major contributions. Each of these advances was accompanied by hard work and disappointments before it began to be economic—but each eventually meant increased efficiency which helped keep low the cost of electricity to the consumer.

The development of nuclear power has followed this pattern, so far, and we expect it will make its economic contribution in the not too distant future. While we were overly optimistic as to the cost of Indian Point when, back in 1955, we decided to build the station, we have learned in our business to be philosophical about engineering obstacles when we are convinced the game is worth the candle. When the United States Congress relaxed the Atomic Energy Act in 1954 and made it possible for private companies to own, build and operate power reactors, we felt that heat from atomic energy could become an economical alternative to the more conventional sources of heat we use—coal, oil and natural gas. We have not changed our minds.

There was no expectation in those early days that Indian Point would produce electricity as cheaply as a conventional plant. The capital costs of the plant have been higher than we expected and operating costs are still unknown. However, the knowledge and the experience which Con Edison has gained in these last few years are some of those intangible benefits on which we expect to collect dividends for many years to come, in the building of nuclear plants that *will* produce economical power. These dividends should be of direct benefit to our customers.

Yet we must be careful that we do not overestimate the extent of the economic returns from the use of atomic energy. The electric power industry has already achieved a high efficiency both in the use of fuel and in methods of transmission and distribution. Close regulation by State and Federal authorities assures the customer a fair price for the energy he consumes.

Atomic power cannot alter this picture as drastically as some observers claim. An atomic reactor can only replace the conventional boiler of the generating plant that—for the Con Edison system—represents about 14 per cent of the investment in equipment to generate and deliver electric power to the customer. In our territory, where the bulk of the power is delivered by underground cables, it costs twice as much to deliver electricity as it does to produce it. Delivery cost cannot be affected by savings at the generating station.

It is reasonable to ask what we do expect to gain by our venture into nuclear power. As in all well-developed industry, the savings we make may be small in themselves, but the volume of our business multiplies even small savings. Con Edison's sales of electricity are approaching 20 billion kilowatt hours a year and we can reasonably expect them to double in ten or twelve years. A saving of one-tenth of a cent per kilowatt hour represents $20,000,000, or more.

In the long run, I am quite optimistic about the economics of nuclear power. As the cost of conventional fuels rises in the future, atomic power should become as cheap as, or cheaper than, electricity produced from coal, oil or natural gas.

Another area where nuclear power can make a major contribution is in the reduction of air pollution. Today, on each coal-burning boiler of the size presently purchased, we must spend over $5 million on air-pollution prevention equipment. A nuclear station could eliminate this expense entirely—and the present troublesome air pollution as well. As our country becomes more and more urbanized, the pressure for electric stations that add substantially no pollutants to the air may be expected to increase.

Today these savings and contributions are still in the future. But the future has a way of becoming the present, and you may be interested in some of the steps we have made toward that future as we have built Indian Point.

Con Edison began studying nuclear power in 1952 as a member of the Detroit Edison-Dow Chemical study group (now known as Atomic Power Development Associates), but our study had to take quite a different tack in 1954 when we began to think about actually building a power plant. We approached the job in much the same way as a conventional plant: we asked manufacturers to make proposals that we could evaluate. We chose a pressurized-water, uranium-thorium converter reactor as proposed by The Babcock & Wilcox Company. We added conventional oil-fired superheaters to boost the temperature of the steam from 450° up to 1000°; this permits us to use more efficient turbines. The use of thorium as well as uranium in a power reactor appealed to us as a way to make a major contribution to a developing art.

While the nuclear engineers were wrestling with the problems of reactor design, our structural engineers had to figure out how to provide the necessary shielding for the reactor. It is surprising how many ways this can be done. We considered several before we settled on a design that places all the nuclear steam-generating equipment inside a single, steel *containment sphere* which is surrounded by an external, concrete *biological shield*. The latter is radiation shielding to protect workers and the outside public from radioactivity under any foreseeable conditions. The former is a sealed steel ball strong enough to stop any flying parts and contain radioactive materials even should the maximum credible accident take place in the reactor. This two-layer construction enables us to reduce the size of the steel sphere, and, at the same time, assures our ability to build additional nuclear or conventional units at Indian Point which could be operated safely, even though a serious accident might force one reactor's shutdown. It also protects the public from any undesirable radioactivity during such an accident. We also decided that we would forego access into the shield and containment sphere during normal operation of the reactor, although there will be provision for men to enter the containment for inspection when the reactor is shut down but the system is still at operating temperature and pressure.

It required over two years of study, research and engineering before we were assured that we had a design that would be operable and give us the margins of safety we felt were required by the unknowns of the art of atomic power. In the meantime, the nuclear engineers had designed a fuel element using uranium and thorium in metallic form. But physical tests of this design disclosed a serious defect. Not much was known about thorium in those early days—prior to the atomic age, thorium's principal use had been for the Welsbach mantles of the gaslight era. Tests of metallic thorium fuel elements showed that when a defect occurred in the cladding (casing) and the thorium corroded, the volume of corrosion products was so high that a coolant channel might be blocked, causing a reactor failure. So the engineers started all over again and, using thorium and uranium in oxide forms, came up with the "pin type" of fuel element with the atomic fuel in ceramic form inside of long tubes or pins.

Construction of the 160-foot-diameter steel containment sphere had high priority. At the same time we began construction of the wall of the concrete outer shield, which averages 5½ feet in thickness and rises 90 feet above the foundations. The steel sphere had to be erected and supported as a free-standing ball until it passed a pressure test to make certain there were no leaks. After this, the permanent support was added and concrete foundations for the nuclear equipment poured inside it. The Chicago Bridge and Iron people designed and built the sphere to our specifications. One-inch-thick sections of the steel sphere, properly formed at the mill, were delivered to the site. Here they were welded into larger sections, swung into place, and welded to their neighbors. Each weld was radiographed to detect any hidden flaws.

When the sphere was completed, all the 487 openings through it were sealed, and the sphere was subjected to a 24-hour pressure test to check for leaks. Successful conclusion of this test assured that the sphere could contain the design internal pressure of 25 pounds. Now the blanks covering the equipment hatches were cut away (some were steel plates fifteen feet across)—and the readying of the sphere for the boilers and reactors began.

We now began placing the dome on the concrete outer wall of the shield, which has a diameter of 181 feet. In order that the wall could support the outward thrust of the 7,000-ton dome, the wall was wrapped with almost 300 miles of steel wire under tension, in a trough fifteen feet wide which had been cast in the upper outside circumference of the concrete wall. The dome itself is of pre-cast, pre-stressed concrete fabricated at the site. Each of the 24 ribs which rise from the wall to the compression ring at the top weigh 64 tons. In between are set planks of concrete designed to fit together like a three-dimensional jigsaw puzzle.

Work on the conventional part of the plant also went forward. Foundations for the superheaters, the turbine room, and the screen well-house were poured and the structural steel erected. A DeLong Dock, similar to a Texas Tower, was floated up the Hudson and secured in place. Indian Point was a busy place with often more than a thousand men employed at the site.

The nuclear portion of the plant is the most interesting because it is a new development. Inside the containment vessel, we erected the equivalent of an eleven-story steel structure and poured the concrete housing for the reactor pressure-vessel. This pressure vessel weighs some 266 tons. It stands 38 feet high, has an inside diameter of 9'7". The walls are of carbon steel lined with stainless steel and are 7 inches thick.

The core of the reactor, the heat-producing unit, is being installed inside the vessel. It is always amazing to me that the core, which is about 6 feet square and 9 feet high, can produce enough heat to produce 163,000 kilowatts. Compare this with the superheaters, each of which stands as high as an eleven-story building and is 30 by 35 feet in cross section and produces heat for 56,000 kilowatts.

The explanation lies in the vast amount of energy which can be generated in a small space by nuclear fuel. The Indian Point core is made up of 120 fuel elements, each holding 195 tubes packed with pellets containing uranium-235 oxide and thorium oxide. These tubes are .3 of an inch in outside diameter and have fuel in 98.5 inches of their length. Thus the core has a heating surface of 15,600 square feet.

Water under 1,500 pounds-per-square-inch pressure, pumped at the rate of 133,500 gallons per minute, carries away the heat of the chain reaction within the core. The water gives up its heat to a secondary water system in steam boilers much the way a radiator gives up its heat to air in a room. This arrangement produces non-radioactive steam which then leaves the nuclear portion of the plant, passes through the superheaters and on to the turbine. After the steam has done its work, it is condensed back to water and pumped back to the boilers to pick up more heat.

To keep corrosion to a minimum, the water in these closed systems is highly purified, and it comes in contact only with stainless steel or zirconium (which is known for its corrosion resistance). Indian Point's water purification system provides water with a maximum of one part per million solids and one ppm soluble materials. We had to develop new equipment so that we could measure water of this purity, for, by comparison, New York City water— some of the purest drinking water available anywhere— averages 50 ppm solids and solubles.

The use of special materials, of new techniques and of equipment undreamed of a few years ago, helps explain why these first atomic power plants are so expensive. Practically everything in the nuclear portion of the Indian Point plant is custom made. For example, in cooperation with manufacturers, we have developed a special electrical cable which is impervious to gases passing longitudinally through the insulation. This cable will be used for all circuits that enter the reactor containment and is part of our design to provide gas-tight containment for the reactor. The safety features designed into the plant add considerably to the over-all cost. A book could be written about just the remotely-controlled mixing station where low-level wastes will be packaged in steel and concrete for shipment to disposal areas.

All this care, including the shielding inside the steel sphere and the massive outer shielding, is made necessary by the requirements of the Atomic Energy Commission and by the particular operating requirements we have set for Indian Point. Regulations of the AEC determine the levels of radiation and exposure of workers allowed at the site. These regulations are based on standards established by the National Committee on Radiation Protection and Measurement and by the International Commission on Radiological Protection, two independent bodies of scientists, doctors and biologists and physicists.

The keys to reducing the costs of atomic power lie in experience and standardization. While the industry is not yet ready for the latter, experience is being gained through the design, the construction and the operation of full-scale power reactors. This experience is laying the groundwork for future standardization.

We expect to operate Indian Point as a regular station contributing to our total generating capacity of approximately 5,500,000 kilowatts. Indian Point's 255,000 kilowatt net generating capacity will be less than four per cent of the Company's total capacity; therefore, Indian Point cannot have an appreciable effect on our total financial operations or the cost of electricity to our customers.

Con Edison has built Indian Point without any subsidy from the government. It has been our consistent belief that the true costs of atomic power will be known only if it is developed without benefit of direct subsidies and that an atomic power plant should pay taxes as does any other productive equipment. We feel that without the spur of competition with conventional plants, there will not be the pressure to achieve competitive power costs.

The costs of other Con Edison innovations—the first boiler designed for the use of pulverized coal, the first network-protector for alternating current networks, the first metal-clad switchgear—were far more than one could justify if each of these advances were one of a kind. But, over the long haul what was learned in the early stages of research, design, development, manufacture and installation of these pieces of hardware led to increased efficiencies and to lower costs.

Indian Point and other first-generation power reactors must be viewed in this light. I am sure that in the future, Americans will look upon them as crude prototypes of atomic power stations. But I believe they will also see in them further evidence that electric utilities take seriously their responsibilities to their customers and stockholders to be ready to meet the power demands of the future at the lowest possible cost.

Howard A. Wilcox

the director of research and engineering of the Defense
Systems Division of General Motors, was until 1960 deputy
director of defense research and engineering at The Pentagon.

A nuclear physicist, Dr. Wilcox taught at Minnesota,
Harvard, the University of Chicago, and the University of
California; he was a scientist at the Los Alamos laboratories,
and research physicist and head of guided missile development for the United States Naval Ordnance Test Station,
Inyokern, California. He is a specialist in the penetration
of matter by charged particles, the production of mesons in
proton-proton collisions, and in proton-carbon collision.

CHAPTER FOUR

THE TECHNICAL
INNOVATIONS AND SOCIAL
CHANGE

W<small>E ARE ALL INTERESTED</small> in what the future
has to bring, but thus far we know of no method for making reliable and detailed predictions, except perhaps in
relation to aspects of inanimate nature. Thus far, the laws
obeyed by human individuals and human societies are so
complex that they defy, almost completely, the grasp of
our present understanding. This is true even admitting
the great efforts put forward by such social scientists as
Margaret Mead and Sigmund Freud and such highly tal-
ented amateurs as Karl Marx and Thomas Malthus.

Today it is clear that we are in a period of rapid change,
both technological and social. We often hear it said that
the most permanent feature of man's activity is its ceaseless change, but, in fact, history provides many examples
of societies that existed for hundreds and even thousands
of years with little or no change, for example the Egyptian
and the Chinese dynasties. The present period of rapid
change is almost unique in history, and I doubt that it will
endure for more than one or two hundred years more.

Let us consider the present-day phenomenon of technological innovation and social change. Today, the primary
causes of social innovation seem to be the pressures of
age-old human desires as released by and redirected
through technological advances. These advances have
opened new ways for human beings to fulfill their desires
—desires to love one another, control one another, hate
one another. It would be tempting to say that *all* social
innovation occurs as a result of technological change, but
once again a reading of history demonstrates that this is
not the case. The revolutionary activities of Gautama the
Buddha and of Jesus Christ were not related to technological discoveries. But it *is* valid to say that social changes
tend to come slowly unless they are driven by the pressures
of technological change and the resulting clash of social
systems in conflict.

All these great forces are in action today, and consequently we are adjusting our societies very rapidly. Consider our recent shift from an isolationist viewpoint to a
nearly complete acceptance of the role of leading world
power. Consider the change from a few years ago, when
the prestige of the peacetime military establishment was
low to our present acceptance of a huge peacetime budget
on behalf of the defense of our country and the social
stability of the entire world. In another vein, consider our
acceptance in the last few years of all sorts of affronts to
our habits, privacy, and sense of decency, brought about
through the influence of modern advertising techniques.
Consider that a few years ago we were fighting the American Indian—now we have forgotten him; a few years ago
we were fighting the Japanese—now they are our friends;
not very long ago we hanged witches—now we don't even
admit their existence. A few months ago we were explod-

ing atom bombs for test purposes—now we are half expecting that in some way they will be outlawed.

These examples, and many others, prove to me that today we are rather rapidly changing our social viewpoints and customs, in an attempt to adjust to the new technological possibilities through which our human desires can express themselves. We are attempting to develop laws and taboos and other social safeguards to protect us from the undesirable consequences which have been made newly available to man through the technological advances. If we create adequate social safeguards rapidly enough, we can live very well, for technology has opened to man's vision the possibility of establishing this Earth as a vast garden for his development and his joy. At the same time, technology has made it possible for man to turn the Earth into a vast desert inhabited only, perhaps, by a few surviving plants and insects.

I will try to explore some of the technological possibilities which might be brought to reality in the next hundred years. Most fundamentally, I would point to the possibility that man can have under his control and essentially unlimited quantity of energy. In the days of the Romans a man was rich if he had a few slaves to work for him. Indeed, most men were slaves, rather than slave-owners. Today, every man, woman and child in this country has the equivalent of some twenty slaves to do his bidding. These "slaves" are, of course, the machines and the energy made available by the technological revolution of the last two hundred years.

In the future, we might visualize a powerhouse built on the shore of an ocean. Into one gate of this powerhouse is pumped the seawater. It passes through a series of complex steps and operations, resulting in the separation of that small fraction comprising the heavy isotopes of hydrogen; from another gate in the powerhouse, the remaining ocean water is returned to the deeps. The precious heavy isotopes of hydrogen are caused to undergo a thermonuclear reaction—through devices we presently cannot yet design—but by fundamental laws that *have* been almost completely studied. These laws indicate that a single such powerhouse might well be able to produce in a year more energy than is now used annually by the entire world. It is also not beyond the bounds of technological imagination or possibility to visualize this powerhouse as being completely automatic—and by this I mean it not only would be able to regulate its own operations without the intervention of human hands, but it might even be able to repair itself—to sense when some vital element is about to break down, to alert remedial machines, to extract a replacement element from the stock room, and then to install the replacement for the faulty element.

What an impact on our economic systems and on our value systems, if this dream of unlimited energy at man's disposal, free of labor costs, becomes a reality! And many scientists who have studied this problem say that this vision is not more than one hundred years away from becoming a reality.

Consider next the possibilities of fast personal transportation. We might visualize automobiles that float just above the surface of the earth on an air cushion, capable of speeds up to 300 miles an hour or more. These automobiles would have automatic electronic guidance devices for use on "highways" over both land and the sea, marked out by invisible radar beacons which guide the automobiles along automatically. At three hundred miles an hour one would find it possible to use his automobile to travel almost anywhere in the world in a rather short time. Having arrived at his destination, one would turn off the automatic guidance device and take personal control of the automobile; in that condition the top speed of the automobile might be automatically limited to forty or fifty miles per hour. Since this kind of automobile would be incapable of flight away from a horizontal supporting surface by more than a few feet, one would not need a pilot's license, and manipulation would not be beyond the powers of the average person. The existence of this kind of personal transportation would perhaps spell the doom of the modern big city. It might make men impatient with customs delays at the borders between nations, and so these delays might be eliminated. This kind of personal transportation would enable men to travel throughout the world, perhaps overcoming their prejudices and their mental restrictions to the ideas and thoughts expressed only in their native language.

Another area of important technological improvement will be that of chemistry. Unlimited energy, together with the science of chemistry, makes it probable that man can eventually manufacture all the food he will ever need, no matter how many individuals populate the earth. Unlimited energy plus chemical skill will enable man to manufacture as much gasoline as he may need to power his transportation devices, if, indeed, they are then still running on gasoline. Chemical skill might provide us new forms of "food"—pills, pills which can perhaps cure various forms of insanity. Pills to prevent the conception of children when not desired by the parents. One sort of pills to give one a boy-child, and another sort of pills to give one a girl-child. Pills which might prevent the growth of hair on a man's chin and at the same time promote the growth of hair on his head. Pills which might even— and here I am relying far more on the fact that we do not know it to be impossible than that we know it to be possible—pills which might even prevent or eliminate biological aging and death.

Consider next some of the possibilities inherent in electronic accounting and computing and thinking machines. Even now, such machines could be set up to keep track of and to regulate the gross movements of every individual on earth at all times of the day and night. I, for one, would deplore such an application of these fabulous machines, for it could create the most horribly efficient dictatorship imaginable. Such an application of technology might be foisted on the people, however, under the slogan that it would "make crime impossible," which I suppose it would. Perhaps one could call it a "crime to end all crime."

But the possibilities inherent in these electronic accounting machines go further—some recent experiments point to the possibility that electrodes might be planted in the brain in appropriate locations, with these electrodes in turn connected to tiny radio receivers which might perhaps be embedded permanently inside the human skull. Signals to a whole group of these radio receivers might then be controlled by a large accounting machine. This could perhaps result in thought control and action control of a most direct and detailed kind. If the people of a nation were to desire it, or were even to permit it, this possibility could, I suppose, be applied on a broad scale once the technological facts underlying the appropriate design had been worked out.

Of course, these marvelous electronic machines can do wonderful things *for* man's welfare, as well. It might well be possible, for example, to design a translating telephone, so that one could push a button labeled "Russian," and talk English into the telephone, and have one's words instantly and automatically translated into Russian for one's listener. Then he would reply in Russian and out of the telephone one would hear English. I suppose this development might help to overcome the "language barrier" that we hear so much about. Perhaps we will all one day be wearing invisible hearing aids in our ears—language translating hearing aids.

I could write at length about many other technological possibilities and some of their foreseeable social consequences—of man's ability some day to control the temperature of the Earth; of his forthcoming ability to control the level of the sea; of his ability to prevent hurricanes; of his ability to travel throughout the solar system, and to visit every planet and heavenly body contained therein, except the Sun itself. But let me conclude my discussion of future possibilities by suggesting that man can some day control his own biological evolution as an animal—he can, if he desires, develop a variety of species of man. Today, biologists tell us, only one species of man lives on the earth. The science of biological evolution points to the possibility of selecting and creating various new species with various new human capabilities, both mental and physical.

Let me turn now to some impossibilities. I suppose everyone would agree that I am on far less sure ground to say that something will be *impossible* to achieve in the future; nevertheless, I feel it important to be a little courageous and discuss some things that science tells us will be impossible. The lay world is now somewhat over-sold on the powers of science. People tend to feel that *any* achievement is possible to science. They forget that the very existence of scientific law is a simple statement that some things are regularly and systematically found to be impossible. Our most powerful and most basic scientific generalizations are assertions about what *cannot* be brought to pass in the natural world. So, to put the picture in balance, let me describe some future impossibilities.

First, I think man will never inhabit a satellite in a stellar system other than his native solar system. To do so would impose intolerable travel time and communication difficulties. Even moving at the prodigious speed of a light pulse (which travels to the moon in approximately one second and takes only eight minutes to reach the sun), it would take over four years for a communication signal to reach the sun's nearest known stellar neighbor.

All modern scientists believe the experimental proofs of the claim—embodied in Einstein's theory of relativity—that no signal nor object can move faster than a pulse of light. For several reasons, I believe that no space ship designed by man will ever travel at a speed exceeding 1/1,000th of the speed of light—that is, 11,160 miles per minute. And so, man can never, in my opinion, hope to reach even the nearest stellar neighbor in less than 4,000 years of travel time. This would be a formidable length of time, for man's cultural evolution proceeds to a significant degree in 4,000 years; whole language systems have arisen and become extinct in less than 4,000 years.

A second technological impossibility would be to transport men away from the earth to other planets as rapidly as they can reproduce themselves. Once the earth is full of people, the human family can fill the moon in 5 to 10 years, Mars in 20 to 40 years, Venus in 30 to 60 years. In just a few years from now, therefore, I feel that man will have to reduce his birth-rate to match his death-rate, or else raise his death-rate to match his birth-rate. Science offers no other possibilities.

A third impossibility would be the provision of a one-hundred per cent effective, active military defense of a large target, such as the U.S.A. or the U.S.S.R., against a determined enemy armed with modern weapons. There are so many ways to wage a successful military attack on a large target, and so many of these ways depend on the successful operation of so few people, that no military defense could hope to forestall them all.

With these thoughts as a background, let me now discuss some possible future social structures. I think effective means can and probably will be worked out for policing out of existence the modern weapons of international warfare. I feel that free, open, democratic societies have greater survival powers than dictatorships. Historical examples seem to show that dictatorial societies are too vulnerable to the loss of one or a few individuals to be able to endure for very long. I think it possible that the laws by which our world society governs itself will some day come to be established on the basic needs of man, so that these laws become relatively few and largely self-enforcing.

Of course, before that is possible, men will have to learn that many of the things they value today are ridiculous nonsense, dangerous nonsense, and that these nonsensical things need not and should not be valued. Some of this nonsense is buttressed by men's systems of laws and taboos. It is difficult to get a law repealed once it is written; it is even more difficult to get a society to abandon its taboo system. Indeed, many societies have gone to their deaths in the past simply because they have stubbornly adhered to an overly-rigid and ill-adapted taboo system.

I hope that people may some day learn to value the creativity and the sheer variety inherent in humanity, that people may some day overcome their unreasoning fears of the strange, so that they will refrain from attempting to make everyone else conform to their ideology or die.

In the future, I see it possible that man will have learned how to limit his population level and will have learned how to have everything he desires to satisfy his animal needs, and that his activity may then have much to do with sports, games, painting, music, learning, teaching, entertainment and so forth. I would expect his value concepts to be very different then from what they are today. The idea of wealth and property-status would perhaps cease to be significant, idleness might no longer be a fault of character, thrift would probably be meaningless.

Perhaps a "science of values" will soon arise. I mean by this that we might put various kinds of human groups into isolated, controlled environments and then see what ethical value systems they evolve and how well fitted for survival are the resulting communities. By controlling the environmental parameters of these communities, we might succeed in establishing an empirical basis for a science of social dynamics. Laws giving the rates of change of the intensities of various value concepts as functions of various environmental pressures might be ascertained. From such studies might grow a "science of values" which could in turn lead to the associated profession of "Social Engineer." The emergence of this scientific and engineering discipline would, I hope, enhance man's over-all fitness for survival.

Of course, other far less optimistic social possibilities also exist for the future. Orwell's vision as depicted in his book *1984* could, in fact, be brought to reality. Alternatively, the scientist could become a sort of high priest, denying his teachings and his counsel to other people if he chose. Or a new Dark Age could come about, perhaps as a result of a major war, so that almost all men once again had to struggle to gather or grow at least half-enough food to feed themselves. As Professor Harrison Brown has argued in his book, *The Challenge of Man's Future,* such a Dark Age could become a permanent feature of man's continued existence on earth, for it must be remembered

that man has used up many of the high-grade energy
sources that nature once made available to him in her
original bounty, which he has needed on the long climb
to his present technological and spiritual vantage point.

G. Holmes Perkins

architect, educator and city planner, is professor of architecture and dean of the School of Fine Arts of the University of Pennsylvania.

Mr. Perkins taught architecture and city planning at the University of Michigan and at Harvard where he was Charles Dyer Norton Professor of Regional Planning. He came to the University of Pennsylvania as dean in 1951. He has been consultant to the United Nations and to the British Ministry of Town and Country Planning. He is chairman of the Philadelphia City Planning Commission, and has served on a variety of civic and government planning boards and commissions. He is a fellow of the American Institute of Architects and the author of the *Comparative Outline of Architectural History*.

CHAPTER FIVE

THE PROMISES

Y ESTERDAY'S PROMISES have become today's realities. The scientist has opened a wholly new world by
harnessing energy in amounts and in ways unknown a
generation ago. Now man must learn to utilize the newly
available power. No examination of the impact of the new
technologies has any validity unless we assume that the
new power will be used for peaceful purposes and never
for all-out war. No city, however planned, can be safe for
even a moment against the destructive forces now in the
hands of man. The best defense plans would be obsolete
long before completion. To build for peace is right. To
plan for peace is the only practical and realistic policy.

Our problem is basically twofold. The population explosion is upon us, but even more serious is the necessity
of deciding the kind of environment we want to live in in
the future. The vast reservoir of energy now under man's
control will not of itself insure a finer environment. There
is little evidence from the Industrial Revolution to suggest
that increases in power have made our cities more livable
or attractive. In fact millions of people rebelled against
the ensuing industrial blight and sought sanctuary in the
suburbs—in vain. The problem therefore is not one of
technology. It is not technology that forces us to live amid

decay or in monotonous subdivisions or to exhaust ourselves by daily commuting to work. Indeed, technology
has provided the means to solve these problems. The vision
has been missing. No image of a future utopia has yet
fired the public imagination to the degree that it has the
power to shape decisions.

The scientist has given us the technical means to create
any environment we want. We have the wealth, the power
and the know-how to build the city of our dreams. As to its
form, we have no agreement. There were times, however,
when the harmony of social outlook produced a unity and
beauty which survive to shame us. The limited technical
resources which built Venice and the Italian Hill Towns
show that the basic ingredient is not power or technique
but a soaring imagination. Here are environments to which
we respond with pleasure and excitement hundreds of
years after the death of their architects. The men who
designed these streets and plazas understood the basic
human needs and emotions.

Our primary problem today is not limited to communities modest in size like those of the Middle Ages, when
there were few of much more than 50,000 persons. Instead
we must contend with great and growing metropolitan
regions, such as the Atlantic seacoast from Washington
to Boston. The limits of these regions are not well defined;
their population will probably double during our lifetime;
the physical area of the cities within them will surely
quadruple. Historic maps of the built-up areas of London,
New York, Berlin, Tokyo or any of the great cities of the
world over a 300-year period shows a frightening acceleration of growth; the doubling of the built-up area of London between 1919 and 1939 is typical. By the end of the
19th century the resulting sprawl with its tragic separation
of man from nature sparked the publication of numerous

plans for utopias and cures which, however, were slow in gaining public acceptance.

Man's first instinct was to attempt to escape the smoke and squalor of the city by moving to the country. But the tightly-packed detached houses gave neither privacy nor room for children's play. They provided only temporary escape from high taxes, and seldom offered the convenience of the city. New ideas emerged which gave promise of a better environment, but none of them was designed to cope with the scale of urbanization that lies immediately ahead.

Of all the plans and cures, the most promising was that of an English accountant, Ebenezer Howard, who 60 years ago proposed the Garden City. He recognized the advantages of both concentration and dispersion by proposing the creation of a system of related new towns clustered around a metropolitan core. In this plan, town and country retained their distinctive character and together offered their advantages without their individual drawbacks. The farmer gained a convenient market and the social and cultural attractions of the city; conversely the city dweller, and more particularly his children, had easy access to the pleasures of the countryside. The railroad in those days provided rapid and clean transportation between all the satellites and the center, permitting the preservation of large natural areas open to all. In this sense the inseparable unity of man and nature was recognized. After World War II, the Garden City became the basis of British national planning policy and today fourteen new towns are under construction which mirror the ideals of this pioneer. Nor are such towns confined to Britain; scores of similar towns are being built throughout the world.

In America these ideas were noted and improvements were devised by Henry Wright and Clarence Stein at Rad-

burn and at Greenbelt. Yet nowhere in the United States
did the theory become the basis of planned metropolitan
growth. (It did in post-war London in Sir Patrick Aber-
crombie's plan, all future growth will be limited by a
permanent green belt beyond which new satellite towns
are already being built.)

In Denmark the finger plan of Copenhagen alternates
built-up areas and green open space. The far earlier pro-
posal of Soria y Pata for a Linear City using similar forms
of rapid transit, attempted to achieve many of the same
social objectives. Nor were the goals of Le Corbusier in his
vertical garden city or Wright in Broadacre substantially
different, although the proposed cities assumed astonish-
ingly different forms. All these planning and architectural
ideas are bearing fruit, in the redevelopment of our central business districts and in the broader concepts of some
new developments which begin to display the aspects of a
community—schools, parks and shopping centers—rather
than the aspects of a mere speculative subdivision. The
tendency among the larger and more progressive builders
to stress the social organization of the community mirrors
the preoccupations of earlier theorists with these same
problems. It is out of the utopian proposals that the practical builder derives his current designs. The family, the
neighborhood and the community have become the social
and the architectural building blocks of tomorrow's city.
In such a city, the diverse recreational, educational, cultural and business services demanded by an affluent society
can be offered conveniently and safely.

The Radburn Superblock eloquently restates this principle upon a modest scale. Within the block, families are
drawn together by common interests and activities. On a
larger scale the British New Towns composed of many
neighborhoods, are designed around the needs of the whole

community. The Swedish town of Valingby offers a charm-
ing and far more dramatic variation upon the same theme.
And in Chandigarh, an Indian state's capital grows organically from the same social building blocks.

Although homes occupy more land than all other buildings, the other activities essential to economic and social
health have just as decisive an impact on the form of the
city as it is being built and rebuilt today. Access to each
activity is provided by a system of roads, arterials and
expressways, and by the great parking areas surrounding
each activity. The scale of industry, business, government,
recreation and even of education has combined with the
auto and expressway to create great islands inaccessible
to the pedestrian. Each island is devoted to a single purpose. Our economic system appears to promote such concentrations for reasons of so-called efficiency with few
questions asked as to their social desirability. All the evidence suggests that these islands set in a sea of parked
cars are to be the non-residential units in the future city,
unless more humane and satisfying alternatives are designed by architects and demanded by the public.

Lest this danger appear unreal, let us examine some of
the most recent, presumably the most efficient, and certainly the most widely-heralded projects which are setting
the pattern for tomorrow. In an air photo, it is sometimes
difficult to distinguish one from another: the ball park,
the regional shopping center, the Pentagon, the General
Motors Technical Center, the Connecticut General Life
Insurance offices or some new industrial park. All are
served by expressways and surrounded by parked cars.
Differing only slightly are the proposed Central Business
Districts, the great universities, both urban and suburban,
the central high schools, the governmental centers built

in New Orleans or proposed in Boston, or such cultural concentrations as Lincoln Center.

Each has become a world of its own. Each is a small oasis surrounded by thousands and thousands of cars. Great swaths, 300 to 600 feet wide, without access to the abutting land, cut the region into pieces. Each has been conceived as a unit whose average size and cost is far greater than the normal project of earlier times. Such undertakings are made possible by improved building technology, by massive concentrations of funds and by the use of land in the center of the city assembled through the urban-redevelopment power of eminent domain. Both private and public projects grow larger. Their scale has become so frightening and inhuman that we are driven to seek solitude, friends and release from tension by moving to the small town; we have been pushed out of the city where we are hardly better than unwelcome visitors. Unfortunately there is no escape, for the metropolis has overrun the surrounding region. Only by a re-examination of the principles of city-building will we create an environment capable of sustaining society, where the land has been recaptured for the people from buildings and the automobile.

Size is only a part of the problem. The major question confronting us is what type of environment do we want? Though we have the technology and means to build whatever we choose, architects have seldom recognized that we are confronted by a new scale of thinking. The boldest essays of Wright and Le Corbusier were limited to discreet architectural designs conceived as centers in the larger and neglected landscape. Yesterday there was room for such cities; tomorrow the region will become the unit for design. Town and country, for good or ill, will be irrevocably married.

We are entering a period that will see a metamorphosis of the present metropolis into a balanced ecological region composed of a galaxy of new towns set in a natural environment and connected by a system of expressways and mass transit that will make all parts of the region as accessible as the parts of a small town. Tomorrow, the Lincoln Center and the Metropolitan Museum of Art will be as accessible to the man from Vermont or Maryland as to the New Yorker today. The freedom, the variety of choice, the richness of experience can be incomparably greater than anything ever dreamed of. If we would achieve these goals we need some basic principles to guide us. I would suggest, in the design of the regional city, that the first principle be *adaptability to change,* the recognition that cities are ceaselessly renewing themselves in an organically changing pattern. The second principle must be *freedom of choice,* the recognition of the desirability of the widest possible choice of homes, of jobs, of recreation and of education. This will give greater variety and richness to our lives, and to our architecture, than can be gained by any artificial means. As human beings there are certain eternal values which we cherish, to meet our fellow men and join with them in various activities, also at times to be by ourselves and commune with the inner man. The basic, natural needs of the human being must be satisfied, and these are not to be satisfied by improvement in technology or ease of movement from one place to another. Each region should provide the opportunity for both young and old to live a *balanced life* and to enjoy the pleasures and stimulations of the urban world as well as the world of nature. It should be possible for people to be creative artists or participating athletes, and at other times to be observers. Only in this way can decisive weight be given to social values, both in the extension of present cities and in the redevelopment of their worn-out cores. The fourth principle must be *unity with nature,* acknowledgment that man is an organic element of nature and that his future depends on his ability to contribute to the self-renewing process of the universe and in so doing to abandon his historic role as a parasitic consumer of nature's bounty.

The regional city so conceived will provide freedom with responsibility, richness and contrast, variety and change and, as in nature, constant renewal to meet the new demands of future generations. Though it will be an efficient machine built with the latest technical means, it will serve rather than dominate its citizens. Nor will our plans deal solely with economics, social security and physical health for in the words of Huxley, "This material approach is frankly not enough; however adequately it deals with the foundations of life, it leaves out all its upper stories. Our new view of human destiny insists that emotional and intellectual and spiritual satisfactions must be taken into account."

Merril Eisenbud

is professor of industrial medicine and director of the Environmental Radiation Laboratory of the Institute of Industrial Medicine at New York University Medical Center.

Dr. Eisenbud has held various posts with the U.S. Atomic Energy Commission since 1947, and is currently an A.E.C. consultant. He has served on more than a dozen committees and commissions concerned with radiation and radiation hazard—for the United Nations, the United States, and the New York state and city governments.

He is presently a member of the Expert Advisory Panel on Radiation of the World Health Organization, an alternate United States representative to the United Nations Scientific Committee on the Effects of Atomic Radiation, and a member of the board of directors of the American Nuclear Society.

CHAPTER SIX

THE RISKS

IN THE PROFESSION of radiological hygiene, I find myself in a rather uncomfortable position. I spent fifteen or eighteen years trying to convince people that they had to do something about radiation hazard, but since the pendulum has swung the other way in the last few years, I have found myself trying to induce people to be less panicky about hazard. I alienated half of my friends in the first period and the other half in the second, and for the time being I am in the middle and very much alone.

One of the things most people don't realize is that mankind has always been exposed to radioactivity in very substantial amounts. Radiation and radioactivity were not born with the splitting of the atom in 1942; radioactivity has always been a fundamental property of the world in which we live. Radiation comes from outer space in the form of cosmic rays, which bombard the earth and everyone on it. Radiation comes from the crust of the earth—from uranium, radium, thorium and a number of other elements, including an isotope of the very common element, potassium. If you weigh 150 pounds, the radioactive potassium in your body undergoes about 250,000 disintegrations each minute. Radioactive elements in the soil behave like other chemical elements and are absorbed from the ground by plants, eventually finding their way into our bodies. But the phenomenon of natural radioactivity was formerly little noticed, because there were no instruments generally available to measure it. Nowadays, nearly every schoolboy on the Colorado Plateau is running around with a Geiger counter looking for uranium ore. Many Americans have become aware of natural radioactivity.

X rays, cosmic rays and the radiations from radioactive substances are all called ionizing radiations. Both X rays and radioactivity were discovered around the turn of the century, and their early use resulted in many tragedies. For example, one of the first X-ray photographs was of a man's head, and with the low-energy equipment and slow photographic film then used, a relatively long exposure was required. In that very simple experiment, the first recorded radiation injury seems to have been the loss of hair from the excessive radiation received. This type of experimentation soon resulted in burns and, afterwards it was found that the sites of some of these skin burns developed cancers.

Later, just prior to World War I, it was observed that if one mixed small amounts of radium compounds with zinc sulphide, a powder was obtained that glowed in the dark. It became common practice to use such radium paints for clock dials, and the radium-dial industry mushroomed to meet the wartime need for luminous instrument dials. Those were the days of miserable conditions in workshops. Dial painters were girls paid by the number of dials completed; they worked with little supervision. In order to work faster, the girls would point the brushes with their lips and thus ingest the radioactive chemicals. Later they began to develop bone cancer. About forty-five of the original group of radium dial painters in one New Jersey factory have died of cancer or allied diseases.

However, there were almost eight hundred employees in that group, and until very recently nobody wondered about the ones who did not die. A study is now under way by the New Jersey Department of Health to find the balance of those eight hundred girls. About two hundred and fifty have already been located, women now in their early sixties, many of whom have agreed to come to New York University for radiation measurements. We are finding that many have had substantial amounts of active radium in their bodies for years. One of the many fascinating questions remaining to be answered is why some persons who have been exposed to heavy doses of radiations are not adversely affected, while others die.

Because cancer from radioactivity takes many years to develop, it was not until the early 1930's that this phenomenon really attracted attention. The studies of the dial painters established the concept that small amounts of radioactivity inside the body can produce cancer and, if more than a certain amount of radium lodges in the skeleton, bone cancer may develop. In 1940, just before World War II, recommendations were published concerning the maximum permissible exposure to radium. This important datum, derived from studies of the dial painters, has served as the most fundamental bench mark for the control of radiation hazard: a tenth of a microgram of radium (a tenth of a millionth of a gram) is the maximum that is permitted to accumulate in the body of an industrial worker.

With the establishment of this maximum permissible amount, it was possible to design a set of procedures for the Manhattan District, the World War II agency that developed the atomic bomb. Potentially it was a problem of staggering magnitude. In the first forty years following the discovery of radium, more than 100 people died from the effects of only *two pounds* of pure radium that had been extracted from the earth. Now, in the Manhattan District, it was going to be necessary to deal with radioactivity equivalent to thousands of *tons* of radium. The need to handle this much radioactivity, and handle it safely, must have seemed formidable to the people who had to face this problem in 1942. But, by a fortunate historical coincidence, the bench marks for designing safe procedures had become available in 1940 and were ready to be used.

The Manhattan District established a remarkable safety record during the War. An industrial operation involving 100,000 workers was conducted with complete safety. Uranium mining, milling and refining, isotope diffusion and plutonium production took place, yet no one was hurt by the effects of radioactivity. Later, in 1946, there were two fatal accidents at Los Alamos; a third occurred in the same laboratory in 1959. But, by contrast, there were over two hundred people killed throughout the program through *non-radiation accidents,* such as vehicle collisions, construction accidents or other common industrial mishaps.

This being the case, one may summarize the hazard situation as follows: The ionizing radiations are potentially hazardous. Many early mistakes were made through ignorance. But we learned from those early mistakes and we were able to run a very sizeable industry, full of potential accident hazards, with a good safety record, though not a perfect one, for human beings have failings that cause accidents. It is very difficult to eliminate accidents entirely.

Now, having gone 18 years with a record like this, why is there so much apprehension about radiation hazard today, and why is the public fear of radiation hazard probably the greatest single impediment to the development of atomic energy?

I think the answer lies in the popular association of radiation with war, and I am incapable of the eloquence required to fully describe how dreadful radioactivity really would be in time of major war. But as a result of this widely shared awareness of war horrors, we are likely to get a minor crisis any time a sanitation department worker, dumping a garbage can into his truck, finds an empty isotope container which says "Radiation—Danger." This man will probably call his boss, his boss will call the police and perhaps the Fire Department. This alerts reporters from the local newspapers. Soon, everyone is standing in a big circle looking at this empty little jar that says "Radiation—Danger" and no one seems to know what to do. The result —an exaggerated "incident," headlines and a neighborhood stricken with fear of contamination from radioactivity.

Radiation is, after all, a mysterious thing. You cannot see it, you cannot feel it, and yet it can do all kinds of things to you. In sufficient doses it can cause your hair to fall out, it can affect your blood-forming tissues and produce leukemia, it can make you sterile. The latter effect seems to have made quite an impression, particularly on the young people in the atomic energy laboratories. I understand there is a high degree of over-compensation at Oak Ridge and similar locations, where the birth rates are among the highest of any communities in the country.

Newspaper and periodical coverage of news about radiation hazards must improve substantially if we are to achieve correct public understanding of the subject. We have a good example of the magnitude of this problem in the treatment, by one of our leading national magazines, of an accident that occurred a few years ago in Houston, Texas.

The fact is that a series of mistakes was made by several persons, both before and after the accident. An industrial plant was using a radioactive isotope as a source of radiation. The isotope was contained in a capsule which for some reason required modification. In the course of mechanical handling, the capsule was punctured and radioactive dust spilled out. Appropriate first-aid precautions were evidently not taken, and two employees suffered skin burns from contact with the radioactive material. The burns were not unlike chemical burns although radiation burns must be regarded more seriously because skin cancers sometimes develop. The two men who were involved in the accident went home, tracking a little bit of the radioactive material into their living rooms. This was found, because radioactivity can be detected very easily by Geiger counters. (You can detect very small traces of radioactivity in this way, and you can trace radioactivity wherever it goes, even in such small amounts that it is not dangerous.) I do not think any competent person, including the public health people in the city of Houston, really thought that dangerous amounts of radioactivity were tracked into the homes, but there was a community scare. The families that were involved were ostracized by their neighbors. Rugs and furniture were destroyed if any traces of radioactivity were found. Now, after four years, the incident continues to be publicized. We are told that as a result of this accident, the children of the two men are sick, and that their eyes are being affected. I do not know of any properly informed person who believes this story can have any basis in fact, yet it is still being repeated.

If the incident runs the usual full cycle, there will eventually be a statement that, after all, the accident was not quite as bad as had been reported. But in the minds of many persons, the exaggerated impression of the hazardous atom will remain. We have seen this many times; I will cite a few examples of things that have happened in the past few years.

A physician, who worked at a nuclear research laboratory in 1947-48, went to a large Eastern city in 1950 and subsequently died of a mysterious malady. Another doctor, looking at the dead man's history, noted that he had worked in an atomic energy laboratory and concluded that radioactivity might have been involved. He sent a small sample of bone to a local college where a Geiger counter showed that the bone was radioactive. Prominent newspaper headlines the following day stated that the man had died of radiation injury, one of the martyrs of the atomic energy program. Upon investigation, it turned out that the dead man had been the industrial physician at the laboratory *during the period of construction,* when there was not yet any radioactive material there. On rechecking it was discovered that somebody had forgotten to allow for the natural radioactivity which is always found in bone. No *abnormal* amounts of radioactivity were present in the piece of bone put in the Geiger counter. The next day the true story came out in a small note on one of the back pages of the same newspaper that had carried the big headlines.

At an industrial laboratory near the outskirts of New York City, an explosion once resulted from the ignition of three pounds of thorium. Thorium is a relatively innocuous material, very mildly radioactive. It has metallurgical properties that make it useful for a number of things, including welding rods. Its toxicity is much less than that of lead. When this explosion occurred, it seemed as if the whole of New York City—the Fire Department, the Police Department, the press corps—panicked. Police rode about the neighborhood advising mothers to keep the children indoors. People threw their food into the garbage cans. Three hundred firemen reported for emergency medical treatment (and to this day, I am told, there is at least one fireman who believes he is suffering from radiation injuries as a result of the incident). This was front-page news for a week. It resulted in a joint investigation by the New York State Health Department, the Labor Department, and the Atomic Energy Commission. Their statement indicated that *there was no radioactivity hazard at all* in that incident.

I believe that these, and other examples I could give, illustrate the way in which some parts of the press have confused the public understanding of radiation hazard.

Some of you will say, "But there *is* an argument going on among the scientists. What about that? Why is it that the scientists can not agree?" Let us take a little time to discuss the disagreements that seem to exist in the recent controversy over the fallout of strontium-90. Let us first understand what is known about strontium-90 and its hazards, then identify the uncertainties that exist. I am sure you will agree with me that the area of agreement among scientists is much larger than the area of disagreement.

It is known that when an atomic bomb goes off, large amounts of radioactive material are hurled into the upper atmosphere. The most dangerous of these radioactive materials is a substance called strontium-90 (Sr-90) which is very much like radium in its characteristics—and like calcium, a common mineral in bone and other body tissues. When Sr-90 falls to the earth and gets into the soil, it passes into plants, along with the calcium, and we eat it in our foods. All of us now have strontium-90 in our bodies. There is complete agreement about the amount of strontium-90 that has been produced, how much of it is on the ground and how much of it is going into our bodies. There is agreement that if no further tests are conducted, the amount of strontium-90 in the bones of children will be equivalent to about five per cent of natural radioactivity. That is, the customary radioactivity to which the children are already exposed will be increased about five per cent by this new factor, Sr-90. The significance of a difference of this magnitude can be put into perspective by noting that at Washington Heights in northern Manhattan, the natural radioactivity is about *ten per cent* higher than it is in Brooklyn, ten miles away, because Washington Heights rests on igneous rocks that are more radioactive than the sand found in Brooklyn, and because Washington Heights is a couple of hundred feet higher and therefore slightly more exposed to the cosmic rays.

In Denver, Colorado, people are exposed to twice as much natural radiation as New Yorkers. In certain places in Brazil, the natural radioactivity is one hundred times the amount in New York.

Studies are being made of the effects of these abnormally high levels of radioactivity, but this is already clear: the strontium-90 to which we are being exposed has increased our radioactive exposure by only about five per cent, which is much less than the place-to-place variation of the natural radioactivity to which we have *always* been exposed. This being the case, why should we be concerned?

The answer is simply that many scientists believe that any radiation dose, however small, is capable of doing harm.

One learns about these things from either animal experiments or studies of humans and, for practical reasons, one is always limited in the size of the population group that can be studied. Ordinarily, if one is studying the toxicity of a substance to be put into a food, or of a new drug or industrial chemical, an experiment is undertaken with at most a few hundred animals, and when the experiment is completed, it may be concluded that the material is not toxic. But have we really the right to say, flatly: "The substance is not toxic"? Not really. At best, we may conclude that if it *is* toxic, the effects are so minor that they are of no great concern. From a practical point of view, an effect "of no great concern" is one occurring so infrequently that it cannot be detected in a public health survey. If one examines 100,000 people and cannot find specifically that their health has been damaged, one concludes that if there is an injury-producing factor the frequency of injury is so small it cannot be observed. When a risk is that small, individuals are not inclined to be concerned about it. We conclude that the risk is "acceptable." In industry, these are the risks we have learned to take. If we had to design industry so that there were *never* any accidents, our technology would be so complicated and so expensive that we simply could not enjoy its benefits. With respect to the toxicity of substances, we are ordinarily satisfied to reduce injuries to the point where they occur so infrequently that they cannot be observed. We say the hazard is "negligible."

For a few years it was said, "We do not think there is a fallout hazard; the hazard is negligible." Then a new concept came into the picture, which could be a valid concept with implications that go far beyond fallout and radiation. The concept can be illustrated by noting that even if a risk is as small as one in a million, when three billion people are exposed to a risk of one in a million, 3,000 injuries may result.

The United Nations, in a scientific report, concluded that the number of cases of leukemia that would be produced by strontium-90 would vary from zero to something like 2500 per year, all over the world. That is, there is an infinite variation in the number of predictable cases of injury at the very bottom of the dose-response curve. This problem is not unique to radiation effects; it presents itself in regard to food additives. In 1959, near Thanksgiving time, it was realized that one could extrapolate dose-response curves from animal experiments and show that it was possible someone might develop cancer from aminotrizole used as a cranberry spray. The berries were ordered to be taken off the market if the chemical was detectable, without regard to amount. Later, the same problem arose from the use of stilbesterol as an additive to chicken feed. The quantitative thinking that developed in the fallout controversy is now affecting thinking in regard to other problems including air polution and drugs.

If I may be permitted to make a forecast, it is this: in the next decade there will be many controversies of the type that we have had in connection with fallout. Concerning new substances to be introduced into our environment, there will be some who will say, "We did our best; we performed the best laboratory experiments we could design. We could not detect any damage, but, on the other hand, we can not prove that if we did this experiment to 180 million people there would be no damage." A short while ago, people took the attitude that one should not worry about a risk so small that it could not be measured; in the long run, the advantages of the innovation would outweigh the disadvantages, particularly if the disadvantages were on a scale which was immeasurable. This philosophy is being replaced by a more conservative one which may or may not be a good thing.

In our technological society, we have to take chances. We introduce all kinds of new chemicals into industry which in the long run do us a lot of good. And yet we may cause—in fact we probably are causing—new health problems. The rising incidence of lung cancer, leukemia and other diseases may be due to technical innovations. Whether the causes are cigarette smoking or automobile exhausts or something else, at present we do not know. We must do our best to protect our health, but even this may require that we assume a considered risk. Would we wish to deny our communities the use of electricity until we have learned to use it in *absolute* safety?

The genetic risk from radioactivity seems to loom large in the popular mind. It is very difficult to express the genetics problem quantitatively in a way which will be generally understood. I can say that if 180 million people receive a dose of strontium-90, it is possible that a specified number may develop bone cancer—but when one talks about genetic injury, the algebra is more complicated for it becomes necessary to distribute the risk over many generations by a relatively complex system of computation.

In this country we have a population of 180 million. The chromosomes of this population occupy a total volume that is smaller than one aspirin tablet. This is the most precious stuff in existence. Here, in a total mass that weighs a small fraction of an ounce, are the blueprints that will determine what the next generation will look like, how smart they will be, how long they will live, how well they will play bridge, whether they will want to be electricians or sailors. The genetic character of future Americans is contained in these chromosomes.

It has been learned that ionizing radiations produce changes in chromosomes. This was first demonstrated in 1927 in experiments on fruit flies, and has since been studied in small mammals. These changes in chromosomes may result in changes in the characteristics of offspring. In most cases, in order for the chromosomal change to

express itself as a change in the characteristics of a descend-
ant, it is necessary that the altered chromosome be present
in the reproductive cells of both the male and female.
Thus, if ionizing radiations produce a change in, for example, the chromosome that determines the size of the ears,
the immediate offspring of the irradiated person will not
be affected except that they too will inherit the altered
chromosome and will, in time, pass on a similar alteration
to their children. So far, the size of the ears of the descendants has been unaffected. But if by chance one of the
descendants should mate with a person carrying the same
changed chromosomal characteristic, the mutation will
then express itself by producing a hereditary change.
Whether the change is a beneficial one or not depends on
the size of ears in this family in the first place, on a person's
point of view and on the nature of the change.

From the above it can be seen that the rate at which
radiation-caused chromosomal changes produce changes
in the characteristics of the population—depends on the
rate of mixing of chromosomes in the population as well
as a number of other factors. Because this mixing rate is
slow, it may take many generations before a given chromosomal change has an opportunity to express itself as a
hereditary change. Some of the calculations of the numbers
of defects produced by the ionizing radiation from fallout
have been projected for twenty-five thousand years. This
is an exceedingly long time in which to be looking ahead.

One cannot readily demonstrate experimentally whether
small doses of radiation produce genetic changes. Very
much larger doses than those normally encountered by
populations are used to demonstrate genetic changes in
experimental animals. However, there is a theoretical
basis and some experimental evidence for believing that
all radiation, regardless of amount, is capable of producing

genetic change. At small doses, changes may take place
so infrequently that they cannot be observed, but it is
assumed that the changes nevertheless do take place. As
a matter of fact, there is a basis for believing that at least
part of the evolutionary changes that have taken place
throughout all biological history have been due in part
to the ionizing radiations from nature. Believing this, a
person might say, "Look at us! Aren't we a good thing,
and aren't we this way because of radioactivity? Otherwise
we might still be a slime in a pond somewhere! Why is
radioactivity bad?"

I will not attempt to answer the question of whether
it is a good thing that we are as we are. Perhaps we *should*
safeguard against additional radiation because of what a
little more radiation might do to us. Many geneticists
argue that there are a limited number of permutations and
combinations of changes that can take place in chromosomes. Evolutionary doctrine says that when a good change
takes place, it survives because of the principle of survival
of the fittest. If a deleterious change takes place, it ulti-
mately dies out. Thus, most of the beneficial combinations
may have already been tried out, and some scientists—
egotists that they are—say that we have become about as
perfect as we can be and that from here on, any more
mutations would produce only defects. In the minds of
many mothers, who after all are more interested than
anyone else in the welfare of children, born or unborn,
there is fear today about medical X ray and exposure to
radioactivity in any form. Many of these mothers would
be comforted to know that the possible genetic injury
that is being talked about is not an injury to children or
grandchildren, but an injury to the offspring's offspring's
offspring many many generations hence. What will this
injury be? Again, nobody knows. Of the many thousands of

genetic injuries that can be expected over the next several hundred years from normal radioactivity, medical X ray, or fallout, many will result in death of the fetus in a very early stage of development, perhaps in the first two or three cell divisions after conception, death to a microscopic fetus, probably without the knowledge of either parent. In other cases, there might be blond hair in a family where you normally expected dark hair, or perhaps a different shape in ears or premature grayness, or maybe no grayness at all. In a small percentage, real social tragedy might result in the form of individuals predisposed to disease or early aging, or afflicted with some kind of deformity.

As in the case of bone cancer from strontium-90, we should be concerned, not because of our fears as individuals, but because this is a problem that faces Mankind. We should think about the matter and we should do what we reasonably can to reduce radiation exposure. The risk to ourselves is small, but we are justified in being concerned because when the world population is subjected to even a very small risk, a substantial number of injuries will take place.

Much of the apparent difference of opinion among leading figures about the effects of radiation comes from a difference in language. One person says that the risk is negligible: what he means is that the risk being one in a million, or one in ten million, it is so small that the individual is in no great danger. Another person insists the risk is serious, for he notes that a risk of one in a million, applied to a population of three billion, will produce many tragedies. Both are correct, from different points of view.

Weighing the hazards and the benefits, I believe we must conclude that when we deal with radioactive material we are dealing with something that is potentially very dangerous, to us as individuals, and to the human race, but that we have learned a great deal about it. I think that we can learn to control the new risks in the same way that we have learned to deal with fire, with electricity and with other hazards which have been introduced from time to time into our society. We must accept some risks from nuclear energy if we are to enjoy its benefits.

Harry J. Carman

the dean of Columbia College from 1943 to 1950, is an educator with interests almost as broad as mankind's. A dirt farmer in upstate New York, Dr. Carman has also been a member of the National War Labor Board and the New York State Board of Mediation. A former schoolteacher and small-town high school principal, he is currently a trustee of six colleges and universities, and senior educational consultant of the John Hay Whitney Foundation. He is particularly interested in higher education and is a member of the Board of Higher Education of the City of New York; he is equally interested in adult education, and has at various times been associated with the educational work of the Joint Industry Board of the Electrical Industry, the International Ladies' Garment Workers' Union, the Standard Oil Company of New Jersey, the American Manufacturing Company and the New York Adult Education Council.

Dr. Carman has written on subjects as widely varied as medical education, street-railway franchises, scientific farming and American cultural history.

CHAPTER SEVEN

A HUMANIST LOOKS
AT THE NUCLEAR AGE

ENGINEERS, and others interested in the impact of applied science upon mankind, believe that the Nuclear Age will give rise to a series of revolutionary modifications in the economic, social, cultural and political patterns of human society. Whether all of these prophesied changes will result from man's harnessing of the atom, we do not at this moment know. However, history unmistakably reveals that whenever new technological devices are introduced they may, depending upon the use to which they are put, profoundly alter existing institutional arrangements, mores and traditional ways of life. For supporting evidence, one has only to survey the technological changes over the last hundred years in the manufacture of textiles, metals and chemicals, in agriculture, transportation, electronics and office equipment, and in the vast network of communications.

More recently, increasing thousands of human hands and minds have been replaced by electrically operated gadgets and machines. In the vast majority of business enterprises and in many fields of research, automation is a prime feeder to the problem of unemployment. Other examples of technological advance on the traditional patterns of life are unnecessary. That this process of substituting machines for humans has not yet reached its zenith must be evident to anyone acquainted with the history of automation. In this connection, we should not overlook what my colleague, Boris Pregel, has so admirably set forth in the opening chapter of this volume, namely, that with the discovery of apparently unlimited sources of energy, attempts to distribute this energy so that everywhere poverty may be eliminated and peace advanced—will give rise to a multitude of problems resulting from the challenge to current patterns and ways of life.

From a humanistic point of view, it is clear that mankind is already beginning to experience the effects of this major challenge, which promises to grow in both breadth and in intensity. Consequently the pages of this chapter will be devoted principally to this aspect of the Nuclear Age. How will human values be affected? With their greater ability to produce material things more quickly and abundantly and with a minimum of hard labor, people, the world over, will find themselves confronted with the luxury of leisure time: what disposition will they make of this extra dividend of the Nuclear Age? What will happen, psychologically, to individuals when they discover that their labors or services are no longer important to the world nor satisfying to themselves? Will the Nuclear Age affect the decline in the crafts and skilled labor? What effect will it have upon such items as population growth and birth control, family and community structure, thrift, social security and the problem of aging? How will it affect systems of education; what will be its impact upon orthodox religion? Will it warp current ethical standards and ideologies and greatly alter the individual's philosophy of life? And, finally (with the United States primarily in mind), will the Nuclear Age be also an age of fear, anxiety, moral uncertainty, loss of confidence and falterings in moral courage—an age in which a social structure based theoretically on the freedom and dignity of the individual will be replaced by demagoguery and authoritarianism?

The extent to which human values will be affected during the Nuclear Age will depend in large measure upon the character of the values now held by people dwelling in the various areas of the globe, the environmental conditions under which they live, and the nature and extent to which this environment undergoes change. The values now held by a people who place emphasis upon freedom, human worth and dignity of the individual—are very different from the values held by those who dwell within the regimented police state with its almost complete disregard for the individual. The democratic way of life rests upon the assumption that men are rational creatures who have certain capacities and virtues, and who in the majority, are creatures of good will. It is deeply rooted in the loftier aspirations of man and, in the United States, it has been nourished by material conditions of a very favorable nature.

Men of every generation—born into what was for each an imperfect world—have built in their minds ideal worlds, utopias of other times or places in which all has been, may be, or will be, well. The Garden of Eden was one such utopia. Christianity gave men the promise of another utopia with its assurance that the lost golden age of the past could be restored—for the virtuous—beyond the grave. Between the 16th and 18th centuries, Francis Bacon, Sir Thomas More and others conceived of utopias on earth of man's own devising where, by deliberate intention and rational direction, men could indefinitely improve the conditions of their existence. Here they would not be subject to rulers who were not of their choosing. Here the individual, instead of the state or prince, could be deified and given opportunity to exercise his God-given, inalienable rights. Here there would be freedom of thought and speech and conscience. Here there would be freedom of self-government and of occupation. Here, above all else, the worth and dignity and creative capacity of the individual would be recognized.

The discovery of an America rich with unexploited natural resources furnished a kind of ready-made utopia for the poverty-stricken and the oppressed of Europe. To them the New World spelled opportunity for economic and social advancement, religious freedom, self-government and justice. And from the day when the first settler put foot on this continent, the concepts of human freedom and human betterment and happiness—though at times partially choked by the destructive forces of selfishness, corruption, racial and religious ignorance and prejudice and crass materialism—have been the ideological backbone of America. It was this concept of democracy that we associate with the memory of Thomas Jefferson, one of the greatest of Americans. It is not without significance that in devising his own epitaph Jefferson selected, out of all his memorable achievements, three for which he wished to be remembered:

> Here was Buried Thomas Jefferson, Author of the Declaration of Independence, of the Statute of Virginia for Religious Freedom, and Father of the University of Virginia.

These three, taken together with their implications, constitute the warp and woof of Jefferson's social philosophy.

What are freedom's implications for those who enjoy it

and those who seek it, at a time when freedom and free institutions are challenged by regimented statism?

Freedom in a democracy does not mean complete or absolute freedom but, as Professor Algo Henderson of the University of Michigan expresses it, freedom to think, to believe, to disbelieve, to speak, to will, to choose. People are free when they are masters of themselves. We become masters of ourselves when we have learned to utilize fully and creatively our individual abilities—intellectual, physical and emotional. People are not free who are handicapped with unnecessary psychological inhibitions, who are victims of poverty, ignorance and preventable disease, who harbor irrational prejudices against men of other views, cultures or races, or who practice religious bigotry. People are free in the degree to which they possess the tools of learning and techniques of action, the ability to verbalize, to analyze and synthesize, to create, to organize, to administer, who deep in their souls are dedicated to the search for truth, who have the spirit and the will to safeguard the ideals of freedom, justice and fair play. To be free, people must practice as well as give lip service to the Good Neighbor principle which in essence means the recognition of the worth and dignity of each human being regardless of race, color, creed or social status.

The dangers to the American way of life are not all without; rather, the most dangerous are within. They are suspicion, prejudice, bigotry, hate, selfishness, ignorance, corruption, civic irresponsibility and the worship of Mammon. No institution in a free society, whether it be the home, the school, the church or synagogue, business organization, or even the government, can long endure the weakening processes of these poisonous enemies.

To date, man has not made the most of his possibilities. In the process of discovering the nature of the physical world, he has failed to discover himself. His concern has been with the external and mechanistic world—the world, as Lewis Mumford expresses it, of the measurable, the repeatable, the standardizable. The inner world of self, of emotion and feeling, quality and value—the very sources of man's humanness have been either too frequently over-looked or regarded as subjective and, therefore, unreal. Man has been so enslaved with the gadgets and machines with which he has gained control over the physical world that he has lost sight of the things of the spirit. His heaven is a heaven of material things. He has lost sight of those values which give meaning to life.

No one would deny that the discovery of nuclear fission has enormously enhanced the energy resources of the world. No one would deny that if put to good purpose, the new energy could contribute immeasurably to the welfare of mankind. It would be a grave error, however, to con-clude that man's ability to release the energy of the atom is in itself a guarantee that a solution has been found for all the problems confronting mankind now and in the future. Science and technology are not ends in themselves but means to an end. Alone, they cannot remake the world or save man from degradation. No amount of energy or mechanization, unless used rightly, can confer on man spiritual values. Too many of us forget that facts, to be of maximum benefit to man, must be interpreted in the light of human values—social, ethical and aesthetic. Man can be endowed with the latest instruments of physical science but live in a moral jungle. We have only to remember the Nazi exterminations of millions of innocent human beings; we have only to consider the possibilities of atomic and bacteriological annihilation. Although energy is regarded as the basic tool of progress, it is no cure-all for the shortcomings of mankind. Instead of minimizing the use of force to settle disputes between nations, we now think and talk in terms of total war. A more abundant supply of energy has not solved the problem of racial segregation in the southern states of the American Union nor prevented the wave of anti-intellectualism during the post World-War years, the broadside attacks of powerful demagogues, the witch-hunts, loyalty oaths or government investigations.

Science is amoral. It furnishes us with no ethical or moral codes. It merely illumines and affects the material conditions of our existence. In any discussion of the effect of the Nuclear Age on human values, it is well to remember that from the beginning of the Industrial Revolution, our technological advances have outstripped our moral development. Education has kept pace with our rising standard of living—yea, has been largely responsible for its rise—but our standards of life have not kept pace with our standards of living. Perhaps the historian Toynbee is right that "man is ethically unprepared for so great a bounty. In the slower evolution of morals he is still unfit for the tremendous responsibility it entails. The command of nature has been put into his hands before he knows how to command himself." The same point of view was admirably expressed a few years ago by General Omar Bradley when he declared:

> Humanity is in danger of being trapped in this world by its moral adolescence. Our knowledge of science has already outstripped our capacity to control it. We have too many men of science; too few men of God. We have grasped the mystery of the atom and rejected the Sermon on the Mount. Man is stumbling blindly through a spiritual darkness while toying with the precarious secrets of life and death. The world has achieved brilliance without wisdom, power with-

out conscience. Ours is a world of nuclear giants and ethical infants.

Though the basic human values are much the same the world over, the immediate impact of the Nuclear Age is likely to be disturbing and give rise to problems, more in the more advanced and industrialized nations than in the backward areas. Especially this is true of the United States. From its colonial beginnings almost to the end of the 19th century, the majority of people earned their livelihood from farming or occupations closely associated with the land. This long association with the soil tended to emphasize or develop in Americans certain characteristics: hardihood, self-reliance and imagination, skills and inventive genius, and self-reliance. Every husbandman was a manufacturer engaged in grinding grain, making soap and candles, preparing the family meat supply, tanning skins, fabricating nails, harness, hats, shoes, furniture, churns, casks and tools. Every home was a factory. The farmer's daily tinkering, devising, improving and repairing made him invention-conscious. As Emerson in his *Essay on Resources* remarked, farmers had "the power and habit of invention in their brain." As population increased and manufacturing developed on a commercial scale, men merely turned to new purposes the skills and aptitudes that had become second nature.

Agrarian America also put a premium on the habit of work. Ceaseless exertion was the price of survival. Every member of the community must be up and doing. Drones and the slothful were condemned. In one of his lectures to young men, Henry Ward Beecher voiced the general opinion of his countrymen when he asserted that "it would be endless to describe the wiles of idleness—how it creeps upon men, how secretly it mingles with their pursuits, how much time it purloins." After the Civil War, General W. T. Sherman found public occasion to thank God that the overthrow of involuntary servitude enabled the Southern whites at last "to earn an honest living." "I pity the person who doesn't work," said Theodore Roosevelt in 1910. Even today, if a person has no purposeful work he is regarded by many as a social parasite. Probably no legacy of our farmer forebears has entered more deeply into our national psychology than devotion to work.

The worship of work rendered it difficult for many Americans to enjoy leisure. Moreover, this attachment to useful work has contributed in some degree to aesthetic considerations. For many, beauty has nothing to contribute to the stern business of living. My point is illustrated by the story of the farmer who was passing a college campus. It irritated him to see "young loafers" wasting their time learning Latin and Greek and reading books that were written before his grandfather was born. Not one of them, not even the faculty, the farmer asserted, knew how to do anything useful; he had tested them out. He had asked the Professor of Greek how many feet of lumber could be sawed from a log 23 inches in diameter and 20 feet long and the professor did not know!

The impact of the Nuclear Age upon the traditional way of life in the United States has already given rise to a number of perplexing problems and to changes in outlook and attitude for many Americans. From a humanistic point of view, three of these problems, in my opinion, are outstanding. These are: (1) unemployment and leisure, (2) religion, and (3) education. To each of these I shall address myself briefly.

Unemployment may be occasioned by illness, incompetence, age, increase in population and labor supply, seasonal fluctuations, cyclical changes and technology. In recent years, automation and cyclical depression have been chiefly responsible for unemployment; automation tends to be increasingly responsible. The mere numbers of those displaced by mechanization fail to disclose the entire story of what this means. The skilled craftsman who derived not only a living but a wide range of satisfactions from his work now finds himself a kind of surplus person, unwarranted and unimportant. He may turn to some other pursuit that may earn him a living but the psychological rewards that were his may no longer derive. And the same may be true of the aging whose greatest joys were those derived from their work. Especially is this true of those who are without a hobby or some other interest to which to turn; not by their own choice, they now have leisure time. To these numbers should be added the armies of wage-earners who have holidays and vacation periods unheard of fifty years ago. In a word, we are increasingly having leisure time which the Nuclear Age promises to increase rather than diminish. Indeed, one of our most challenging problems of the present is the question of how our increasing leisure time can best be utilized. In terms of human values it can be squandered, or it can be used for the intellectual enrichment and ennoblement of mankind.

The whole educational process of this country is undergoing re-examination. The great revolutionary changes which the world is experiencing have made this imperative. Upon the effectiveness of its education system, the future of America depends. In the past, education at all levels has been largely aimed at specific purposes ranging from how to drive a car to preparation for a medical career. Too often, as Dr. Theodore M. Hesburgh, president of Notre Dame University, points out, our institutions of learning have neglected to help the individual discover himself and his strengths and weaknesses. Too often they have failed to liberate him from the bondage of ignorance, prejudice, passion and bigotry, or to expand his knowledge of geography and the world's natural resources, or to broaden his understanding of the historical past. Too little attention has been given to basic values which should constitute the core of any person's education. These include: love of truth in all its forms—scientific, humanistic, philosophical, poetic, theological; perception of the good of man and of society, and some disposition to work courageously to realize that which we know to be good; a love of beauty in all its forms and, conversely, a distaste for that which is blatantly and deliberately ugly; a passion for justice, insofar as we can achieve for others and for ourselves that which is right and just; compassion for those who are less fortunate than ourselves spiritually, educationally, socially and in the civic order of human rights. These are values which make for human dignity and excellence of character.

Our institutions of learning, especially at the higher level, should be centers for the pursuit of truth and the dissemination thereof. Research and teaching are related functions. Without the effort to extend the boundaries of knowledge and understanding, teaching will atrophy. A university should be a place where students learn not merely from the past but also through developing the capacity and habit of independent thought. In our schools and colleges, youth needs to wrestle with social, economic, moral and political problems. They should not avoid controversial issues merely because they are controversial.

The extraordinary advances in science in Communist Russia, especially in its space and missile program, have led many Americans to conclude that the Communists outrank us intellectually and that we need to redouble our efforts to match them in scientific manpower and accomplishment. We forget, as Dr. Abram L. Sachar, president of Brandeis University, said recently, that the ruthless totalitarianism of Russia accounts—in part, at least—for Russia's preeminence in science. The most creative Russian minds, those with rare talent and genius can find no free outlet in politics, in government, in education, in journalism or literature. In all these areas, censorship is so complete and dangerous that the best brains are channelled into the one conduit that leads to freedom and honor: science. The case of Boris Pasternak is striking evidence of this fact.

It would be a sorry day for America and for the free world if the compulsion to keep pace with the Communists in science were to crowd out all the other cultural values that are precious in a democratic society. The Humanities, Social Sciences and the Creative Arts must not be jeopardized by panic or by distorted emphasis. Dr. Sachar is entirely correct in his observation that wisdom is as important as knowledge, and perspective as important as skill. Statesmanship of a high order is required to devise measures that will enable the free world to keep pace with Russia's scientific achievement and at the same time retain fullest perspective for the humane values wherein rests our superiority over the Communist ideology.

Man is beginning to realize that his culture and social organization are not unchanging cosmic processes but are human creations which may be altered. For those who cherish the democratic faith this means that they can, they must, undertake more or less continuing evaluation of their ideas and institutional patterns in terms of the consequences for human life. The task of bringing and keeping a culture up-to-date is gigantic, but unless man has the wisdom and courage to undertake this, he cannot be the master of his destiny. In this connection I am reminded of the wise admonition of the philosopher, Alfred North Whitehead, that a people preserves its vigor only so long as it harbors a real contrast between what has been and what may be and is nerved to adventure beyond the safeties of the past. Once such a spirit of venture is lost, a civilization is in full decay. The Nuclear Age, we increasingly realize, is an age of rapid historical transformation. All over the world, old institutions, old traditions and old ways of life are either disintegrating or being outmoded. There are persons who do not comprehend that we are in the midst of a revolution or, knowing it, prefer to ignore its existence. Many of us dislike change and fear it, either because we are accustomed to the habitual or traditional or because change endangers that which is dear to us.

Prophecy is poor history. What the end product will be of the great transformation through which we are passing, no one knows with certainty. Much will depend, it seems to me, upon the direction in which the present revolution is channeled—whether into authoritarian and totalitarian or into democratic channels. If the latter, with its emphasis on a broad spectrum of human welfare, then it seems reasonably certain that the World of Tomorrow may well be a planet whose inhabitants, though continuing to be motivated in part by economic motives, will be primarily dedicated to using their talent and resources, including nuclear energy, to the elimination of poverty, ignorance and all the other forces which enslave and degrade mankind.

They must remember that mere knowledge is not enough, that ethical attitudes and civilized behavior must be wedded to man's control over the physical universe.

My thought on this item is admirably expressed by David Lilienthal, one of America's distinguished spokesmen:

> Greater knowledge about the world, this will, I think, be the keynote of the immediate future. But greater knowledge alone will not be enough. There must also be greater love and understanding among men. And there must also be greater faith, faith in humankind, and faith in the purpose of the creator of the Universe. Knowledge, love, faith, with these three the Atomic Age, the age in which you shall live, can become an age of mercy, of joy and of hope, one of the blessed periods of all history.

SOME CONCLUSIONS

It WAS A TEMPTATION for the editors to pick a single, obvious lesson concerning the Nuclear Age and develop it into a theme for the concluding chapter. The fact is that there is no single lesson, no easy conclusion.

This age resembles the end of the 15th century, when Columbus and his fellow explorers were opening a new world of limitless horizons. The accepted knowledge of the time, "the conventional wisdom," was shaken. Everything from religion to commerce to boundaries of ideas had to be re-evaluated and refitted to the new discoveries. So it is today. Perhaps then, as now, men gathered in the coffee houses to talk of despair and of the smallness of human beings. Nevertheless the world went on evolving and developing. It will continue to do so.

We have been accustomed to a sedately paced evolution which permitted mankind to think about what was happening, so that the institutions of society could slowly adjust. Occasionally this pattern has been interrupted by Columbuses. Today's Columbuses are the teams of scientists; the sailors who implement the discoveries are the engineering technicians.

In the present age of discovery, we have moved ahead so quickly that we have the opportunity of changing almost everything we do, at once. This is wonderful, perhaps too wonderful for all men to comprehend or enjoy. The reactions of many to too rapid change are uneasiness, depression, suspicion, distrust, confusion, disbelief or rejection, in varying degrees. Change is inevitable, of course. It is the present rate of change that is bewildering, and to some men terrifying.

The first and most important problem of the Nuclear Age is peace. We must learn to get along with people who have different ideas, languages, names, colors and religions than our own. We must understand the people of the world and avoid nuclear warfare.

The second problem is LBT, the *lag behind technology*. Technical innovation almost always creates disorder, which persists until new social machinery is developed. This is the lag. Many times before, there have been LBT's. Man has tolerated them as the unavoidable price of progress.

However, as we move ahead in the Nuclear Age, we shall find the LBT problem heightened. The technological speed-up of the Nuclear Age, on top of a pace already speeded since World War II, can be expected to produce more drastic changes and swifter ones than society has ever experienced. As the capacity for innovation is accelerated, the probability of LBT is immensely increased. The challenge will be to accelerate the social and governmental processes so that the disorder of the LBT does not overwhelm us.

In dealing with the problems of the Nuclear Age we must recognize that the Things of the Nuclear Age are not the key to the future. The contributors to this volume have made this point repeatedly: only things in their societal setting have meaning. Consider one example: the automobile. Although seemingly convenient for transporting men and goods, in the city the automobile has become a movement-strangling, air-polluting, space-consuming monster that we are unable to master. If today's 65 million automobiles become 100 million tomorrow, their meaningfulness will depend not on the cars but upon whether we can find roads to move on and places to park. To recognize the difference between things, and things as they are used, is the beginning of Nuclear Age understanding.

The paradoxes of the Nuclear Age must be recognized, too. One of them stems from a basic law of technical change, that even modest innovation may bring on the need for massive reorganization of society. For example, on the island of Java, in Indonesia, rice is customarily harvested one stalk at a time, using a knife so tiny it is almost hidden in the palm of the hand. If the scythe or sickle is substituted, a much smaller labor force will be needed, creating unemployment. The food distribution system among the rural population will be disrupted because rice harvesting is presently done on a crop-sharing basis; the technological improvement will thus deprive entire families of their food supply. Moreover, scythes and sickles are men's implements, and until now it has traditionally been Javanese women who did the harvesting. If the "more efficient" implement is adopted, thirty or forty million rural Javanese will have to work out a completely new system for who does what. In the Nuclear Age, it is reasonable to predict that the widespread technical innovations will necessitate even more complex social and economic reorganizations than this example.

Another paradox is that as cheap nuclear power brings material abundance, the importance of material goods is going to change and in many cases to diminish. When every man can have a car or dishwasher, these items are no longer especially distinctive. The further abundance of such hardware in the future will compel us to find values somewhere else, perhaps through creativity.

Another Nuclear Age paradox is this: in an era characterized by increases in machine efficiency and in teamwork, there is going to be a growing need for individualism. In some of its aspects, Nuclear-Age efficiency threatens to cost us more in lost individual values than it profits society in increased production. The consumer will lose something every time a restaurant is automated so that coffee-dispensing machines replace waitresses who can bid a regular customer "Good morning!" The skilled mechanic will lose when he becomes a mere bolter-on, with no channel for demonstrating his competence. The craftsman will lose when he becomes one of a team of button-pushers, tending the machines that displace his once useful hands. As the technicians promote such automation and production-team activity, increasingly it will be someone else's responsibility to restore and re-create individuality. We shall discuss this point further.

In the Nuclear Age, the technicians will continue to preside over the creation of abundance; that is their function in society. With cheap power available everywhere, we will find ourselves inundated by abundance. The very research processes which blueprint the speedup will themselves partake of automation and acceleration. It is because of this explosion of productivity that the unthinking speak of the future as an age dominated by technicians and engineers. Partly because of the undoubted breadth of influence of technicians and engineers, the best centers of technical education, such as Massachusetts Institute of Technology and The Cooper Union, pay increasing attention to the humanistic education of their students.

Unfortunately, we have no evidence that technicians alone, however broadly educated, will harness what they produce. For technology has a built-in imperative. The engineer who designs outboard motors must make next year's model ten miles-and-hour faster than last year's if he can, and capable of being started by any reasonably bright ten-year-old child. Such "improvement" of design, regardless of its impact, is technology's job. It is Society's job to anticipate what will happen if our waterways are taken over by swarms of ten-year-olds in speeding boats, to consider the dangers, and to forestall them. Perhaps this will be done by engineers educated in the social studies, perhaps by humanists well enough educated in science to anticipate its advances, more likely by a teaming of both humanist and technician. But in the days ahead, by some group of leaders, the accelerated technology must be more strongly directed.

In the Nuclear Age, humanists and social scientists will retain their importance because they possess tools for analysis and prediction of change. Educators will gain in importance, for they will teach society how to cope with the changes. One of the major accelerations of the Nuclear Age will be in the need for re-training. In the past, when a man had finished his formal education, he was not only set for life but he had a craft or profession which, with some outside help, could be passed on to his son. This was true whether he was a physician or a mechanic. But today's physician must go to classes all his life just to keep up with the pace of science. Today's mechanic also goes to school, to keep pace with new materials and new machines. One challenge to the education systems is that they must prepare boys and girls to fill jobs, ten years from now, which have not yet even been invented. (How many high school students, in 1950, were being prepared to be radar operators, programmers, or liquid-oxygen handlers?) Adult education programs, for retraining on an unprecedented scale, appear to be the answer to this problem.

Concurrently, there will be an unprecedented need for nonvocational adult education. Many men and women who work a 30-hour week will enroll in classes to improve their skills in leisure-time activities. In this way they can re-establish the individuality that a push-button job destroyed. Many others will enroll in classes that have no discernible hobbyist or useful application; they will seek education purely for the joy of learning. This is the basis for most of the adult education program at The Cooper Union, and we see the Nuclear Age as a time when engineers will increase the workload and importance of adult-educators.

With provisions from the technicians, pilotage from the social scientists and training from the educators, the organization for the voyage into the Nuclear Age is almost complete. But one more element is needed: Goals and values.

Our present value system is like a Model-T Ford which though still capable of moving has really been made obsolete by technological change. Until now, most of our values have been inextricably bound to scarcity and its alleviation. A man labored eight hours a day to feed and clothe his children; his incentive was survival. A prudent man worked overtime to save, to educate his children so that they might earn a decent living; he was motivated by the scarcity of good jobs. A charitable man sacrificed some of his scarce earnings, possibly a tithe, which his church passed on to the needy. In the Nuclear Age of Abundance, these and many other aspects of our value system will have to be re-assessed.

A family's home is no longer the fruit of years of saving; it represents just a small down payment and a convenient carrying charge. We are witnessing the diminution of the spiritual values of thrift, planning and working-together for material goals. In tomorrow's abundance, these values will have disappeared. What is likely to be left is a strange coupling, a continuation of materialism with a devaluation of the idea of working hard in order to get the material things. Merchants and merchandisers have attempted to substitute a synthetic value-system, based not on any scarcity of the useful, but on a scarcity of the modish. This is the status-symbol idea; it has not noticeably improved the moral tone of American life. For new values, ideals and goals, in the Nuclear Age, we shall have to turn, as we have always done, to the philosophers and religious thinkers and humanitarians. Their work still lies ahead.

We have in prospect a Nuclear Age of unprecedented material abundance, yet an age in which society will be threatened by disruption, the individual by devaluation. If the technology is uncontrolled, then the disorders will overshadow the benefits and the Nuclear Age will be an automated hell. But if man can master those threats, the abundance promises a dream world which can be there when we wake tomorrow. These are our alternatives for the Nuclear Age.

GLOSSARY

What do the technical terms in this book mean?

Atom—the smallest particle of matter that has specific chemical and physical properties. At least 96 different varieties of atom, called *elements,* have been identified. Each atom consists of a nucleus and one or more orbiting electrons.

Atomic power—see *nuclear power.*

Atomic weight—relative weight of the atom of an element, compared with oxygen which has a weight of exactly 16. The notation "uranium-235" refers to uranium with atoms of a relative weight of 235; uranium-238 is a heavier, slightly different uranium with a relative weight of 238. (See also *isotopes.*)

Automation—the automatically controlled operation of a process or apparatus.

Beta particle—see *electron.*

Bombard—to cause rays or particles to strike a target.

Breeder reactor—see *reactor.*

Chain reaction—a reaction of the nucleus of atoms, yielding energy and neutrons which cause further reactions of the same kind, thus becoming self-sustaining as long as the starting material holds out.

Containment—the physical means for containing radiation and possible accident-products at a reactor; also, the process of containing such potentially dangerous materials.

Control rods—rods of a material that absorbs or stops neutrons. In a reactor, these are placed between the tubes that contain the uranium, to regulate the chain reaction.

Cosmic ray—certain rays of extremely high penetrating power, akin to X rays, which come from outer space and continually bombard the earth.

Electron—a very small particle with a negative electrical charge. Electrons are constituents of atoms. *Cathode radiation* (in radio and television tubes), and the *beta radiation* given off by uranium and other radioactive materials, consist of electrons.

Element—see *atom.*

Energy—the capacity to do work.

Enrichment—increase of the proportion of fissionable U-235 in a uranium compound. See *uranium.*

Fallout—the descent through the atmosphere of radioactive particles resulting from a nuclear explosion.

Fission—splitting of an atom's nucleus, thus forming two or more lighter atoms, accompanied by the release—in the form of heat or radiation—of some of the energy that held the original atom together. Atoms which are capable of being split in this way are said to be *fissionable.*

Fusion—a reaction in which two lightweight atoms are fused to form a larger atom, with the release of energy.

Gamma ray—high-energy rays, similar to X rays, given off during some nuclear reactions.

Geiger counter—a device which detects and measures the intensity of radiation.

Generator—a machine that converts mechanical energy into electricity.

Go critical—for a reactor to reach the state where a chain reaction is supported.

Hydrogen—the lightest and simplest element. Ordinary hydrogen atoms consist of one proton in the nucleus and one orbiting electron. Atoms of *heavy hydrogen* or *deuterium* consist of one proton, one neutron and one electron. A third form of the element, called *tritium,* has

atoms consisting of one electron, one proton and two
neutrons.

Ionizing radiation—see *radiation.*

Isotopes—different forms of an element having different numbers of neutrons in the nucleus but the same number
of protons and electrons. Thus they have the same
chemical properties but different atomic weights and often
different properties with reference to radioactivity.

Kilowatt—a unit of electric power, equal to 1000 watts. A
larger unit, the *megawatt,* equals 1000 kilowatts. A *kilowatt-hour* is a unit of work, the amount performed by one
kilowatt acting for an hour.

Moderator—a substance used to slow the neutrons freed by
atomic fission, to a manageable and useful speed. Water
or graphite is commonly used.

Neutron—an uncharged particle, one of the components of
the nucleus of most kinds of atoms.

Nuclear power—power generated by harnessing the energy
released when an atom is broken apart (fission) or when
two atoms are joined together (fusion). Because such
energy is released from the nucleus of the atom, this book
prefers the term *nuclear power* to *atomic power.* Since
nuclear power is generally transmitted as electricity to
where it can be used, the term *nuclear power* also means
electricity that was generated by harnessing the heat of
nuclear reactions.

Nucleus—the dense central portion of an atom, composed
of positively charged *protons* and uncharged *neutrons.*
Ordinary hydrogen, the lightest atom, has a very simple
nucleus consisting of a single proton.

Plutonium—an artificially produced, heavy, fissionable, radioactive, metallic element, formed by bombarding uranium-
238 with neutrons.

Power—energy that is either available to do work or is already so applied.

Proton—a particle with a positive charge, occurring in the
nucleus of every kind of atom.

Radiation—generally, energy and streams of particles or rays emitted by molecules and atoms. *Ionizing radiation* is a kind of radiation which may change the electrical balance of a molecule or atom and may thus break up the particle or change its character or behavior.

Radioactivity—the property of certain atoms (including those of the elements radium, uranium, thorium and plutonium) to spontaneously emit rays or particles.

Radium—an intensely radioactive heavy metal. It was the first element whose radioactive properties were systematically studied.

Reactor—an apparatus in which a controlled, nuclear chain-reaction takes place. Reactors produce heat and radiation, and some reactors are designed to produce artificial fissionable elements such as plutonium or U-233. A *breeder reactor* produces more fissionable materials than it consumes.

Shielding—protection; in this book the term means protection from radiation.

Strontium—a fairly heavy metal, chemically similar to the common calcium that is found in chalk, limestone, milk and animal bone structures. When an atomic bomb is exploded, quantities of a radioactive isotope of strontium, *strontium-90,* are formed.

Superheater—in electric power terminology, a device which imparts additional heat to steam that has already been generated in a boiler.

Thermonuclear—related to changes in the nucleus of a very light atom, generally hydrogen or helium. These changes require very high temperatures to start them, as in the hydrogen bomb, a thermonuclear weapon.

Thorium—a very heavy, radioactive element. On bombardment in a reactor, thorium-232 is converted to usefully fissionable uranium-233.

Tritium—an isotope of the element hydrogen.

Turbine—a machine which converts a flow of steam or water

into rotary motion capable of turning an electric generator.

Uranium—a very heavy, radioactive metal. When found in nature, uranium consists of a mixture of three isotopes, uranium-238 (or U-238), uranium-235, and a minute trace of uranium-234. U-235 is fissionable. U-238 can be converted to plutonium which is fissionable. Thus uranium is the starting point for nuclear fission processes.

X *ray*—a form of radiation, generated in a special kind of vacuum tube and widely used for medical purposes and certain industrial processes.

Zirconium—a very tough metal, related to titanium. A patented alloy called *Zircaloy* can be used for the tubes that contain the radioactive materials in reactors.

BIBLIOGRAPHY AND SUGGESTIONS
FOR FURTHER READING

No reading list can be complete, for whole libraries exist devoted to nuclear science, to power technology and to social philosophy. What follows is an annotated bibliography broken down into eight categories, to guide down some of the paths of further study those whose interest has been encouraged by the chapters in this volume.

THE GENERAL PROBLEM

Atomic Industrial Forum.
Atomic energy; the new industrial frontier. The Forum, New York, 1955.
A collection of the proceedings of a two-day forum meeting jointly sponsored with Stanford Research Institute. Papers on food and agriculture, specialized uses of reactors, reactor safety considerations, nuclear fuels and various other industrial-use topics.

Brown, Harrison.
The challenge of man's future. Viking, New York, 1954.
A survey of the diverse fields of man's knowledge, built into a challenging discussion of how the problems of energy, food, raw materials and population are interdependent.

Dean, Gordon E.

Report on the atom; what you should know about the atomic energy program of the United States. Knopf, New York, 1953.

Addressed primarily to the people of the United States by a former chairman of the United States Atomic Energy Commission. Describes the methods and goals of this nation's atomic energy program. The mining and processing of uranium, the atomic bomb, radio-isotopes and the potentials of nuclear power are discussed authoritatively and in non-technical terminology.

Hughes, Donald James.

On nuclear energy; its potential for peacetime uses. Harvard University Press, Cambridge, 1957.

The author first introduces the reader to the fundamentals of atomic and nuclear physics and then leads him through a series of steps to reactor physics and engineering. He also treats some of the problems involved in the nonmilitary applications of fusion. There is also a discussion of the economic and political aspects involved in the peacetime applications of nuclear physics.

Lang, Daniel.

The man in the thick lead suit. Oxford, New York, 1954.

A group of articles reprinted from the *New Yorker.* They are portraits of some of the men connected with atomic development, and observations on their work.

Laurence, William Leonard.

Men and atoms; the discovery, the uses, and the future of atomic energy. Simon and Schuster, New York, 1959.

The A-bombing expedition over Nagasaki is one of the highlights of this book, which also takes the reader back to early discoveries that led to the atomic bomb, tells why the Germans missed building the weapon and outlines a coming new world that the atom is creating, in which, Laurence maintains, war is doomed.

Teller, Edward, and Latter, Albert L.

Our nuclear future; facts, dangers and opportunities. Criterion, New York, 1958.

Tells as simply as possible the problems and opportunities of atomic physics and the dangers of radioactive fallout. Drs. Teller and Latter have written for the layman a book which gives the background usually presented in more advanced and comprehensive treatises.

PEACEFUL USES OF NUCLEAR ENERGY

Akademiia nauk USSR.

Conference of the Academy of Sciences of the USSR on the peaceful uses of atomic energy, July 1-5, 1955 . . . in English translation . . . U.S. Atomic Energy Commission, Washington, 1956. 4 v.

This conference took place just before the United Nations Conference at Geneva on the same subject; it does not contain any papers which were to be presented there. V. 3, contains the introductory remarks and the session of the division of physical and mathematical sciences. V. 1, contains the session of the division of technical science, V. 2, the session of the division of biological science, and V. 4, the session of the division of chemical science.

Allardice, Corbin, ed.

Atomic power; an appraisal. Pergamon, New York, 1957.

A panel discussion presented to the Eleventh Annual Meeting of the Board of Governors of the World Bank. Eight introductory chapters. Two are elementary and deal with the basic introduction to atoms and atomic energy; five deal with the uses of radioisotopes and the types and uses of various reactors; one is on the economics of nuclear power.

American Management Association.

Profit perspectives in atomic energy; problems and opportunities. Elizabeth Marting, editor. The Association, New York, 1957. (special report, no. 21)

The special AMA conference on "Managing the Atom," February 7-8, 1957, designed to help management meet the challenge of the race to apply atomic power commercially. Report highlights what leading companies in the field are doing towards solving problems in the areas of return on investment, government regulation, hazards and their insurance, and manpower and technology.

Fearnside, K. (and others).
Applied atomic energy. Temple Press, London, 1951.
Deals in brief but yet concise form with the application of atomic energy to peaceful purposes. Provides the basic knowledge of nuclear physics necessary to an understanding of the advantages to be derived from new techniques. Of great interest to scientists working in other fields, to the intelligent layman and to the student.

Isard, Walter, and Whitney, Vincent.
Atomic power, and economic and social analysis; a study in industrial location and regional economic development. Blakiston, New York, 1952.
An analysis of the economic problems involved in peacetime applications of atomic energy. This study is timely and important.

Mason, Edward Sagendorph.
Reports on the productive uses of nuclear energy. National Planning Association, Washington, 1955. 51 p.
This study was originally prepared as a part of the United States contribution to the International Conference on the Peaceful Uses of Atomic Energy held at Geneva, in August of 1955.

Newman, James Roy, and Miller, Byron S.
The control of atomic energy; a study of its social, economic, and political implications. Whittlesey House, New York, 1948.
The first comprehensive work on the Atomic Energy Act of 1946. A well organized annotation of the basic features of this remarkable statute.

Rochman, Arnold.
Introduction to nuclear power costs. Simmons-Boardman, New York, 1959.
This monograph analyzes some of the factors which make up the total cost of nuclear power, and shows how variations in

their value may affect the overall cost structure. Having treated the individual cost factors, the study is then directed to an analysis of existing total power cost estimates. The final sections of the study consist of an analysis of the importance of two major cost factors, and the conclusions which may be drawn from the entire study.

Sacks, Jacob.
The atom at work. Rev. printing. Ronald Press, New York, 1956.
A popular account of progress in the understanding and application of atomic energy and artificial radioactivity. The historical and scientific backgrounds are outlined and atomic piles, radioactive isotopes, the atomic bomb and other potential radioactive weapons, and atomic power are then introduced.

Scientific American (periodical).
Atomic power. Simon and Schuster, New York, 1955. 180 p.
Chapters of this book were first published as articles in *Scientific American.* Book is written for the layman yet its level of presentation is such that it will command attention of the engineer who does not have formal training in nucleonics.

Wendt, Gerald.
Prospects of nuclear power and technology. Van Nostrand, Princeton, 1957.
An excellent job of abstracting the lengthy reports of the United Nations Conference on the Peaceful Uses of Atomic Energy and of putting them in a form which should be readable and interesting to scientist and nonscientist alike. Discusses briefly, simply and completely the technical aspects of producing nuclear power.

NUCLEAR PHYSICS—FOR THE LAYMAN

Bishop, Amasa Stone.
Project Sherwood; the U.S. program in controlled fusion. Prepared for the U.S. Atomic Energy Commission. Addison-Wesley, Reading, Mass., 1958.
The author reviews basic principles of controlled fusion and

then the technical and administrative history of the Sherwood projects. The fundamental ideas and the principal difficulties behind each of the approaches are explained without mathematics. Appendices include tabulations of experimental models and glossaries.

Feinberg, Joseph George.
The atom story; being the story of the storm and the human race. Philosophical Library, New York, 1953.
A comprehensive account which begins with the atomic ideas of the Greeks and ends with the hydrogen bomb. About half of the book is devoted to pre-fission discoveries and ideas, the rest to the discovery of nuclear fission and subsequent developments.

Gamow, George.
Mr. Tompkins explores the atom. Macmillan, New York, 1944. 97 p.
Translates into everyday language the vast store of information now available concerning the components of the atom. Illustrates "Maxwell's demon," behavior of electrons, Pauli-principle, Dirac's electron-ocean, nuclear fissions, the neutrino, etc.

Gaynor, Frank, ed.
Concise encyclopedia of atomic energy. Philosophical Library, New York, 1950.
Presents a comprehensive collection of brief definitions and explanations of the terms in the field of nuclear physics and atomic energy, intended merely to give a general understanding of the atom—its nucleus, its energy and their relationship to human life and progress. Thumbnail biographical sketches of outstanding nuclear physicists and chemists are included.

Hawley, Gessner Goodrich, and Leifson, Sigmund W.
Atomic energy in war and peace. Reinhold, New York, 1945.
Written in a manner easily understandable to even those with the sketchiest background of physics, this book was prepared to provide an essential knowledge of the atomic theory. The first portion is devoted to the atom, neutrons, radioactivity nuclear fission and other subjects of fundamental importance. The second portion gives the story of the atomic bomb project. The

concluding section discusses future military and industrial applications of atomic energy.

Helvey, T. C.
Effects of nuclear radiation on men and materials. J. F. Rider, New York, 1959. 56 p.
This short book presents some of the basic principles and data on the physicochemical effects of radiation. Explains those physics which are important in this field. Written primarily for the design engineer of a nuclear powered vehicle, but interesting and elementary enough for the layman. Illustrations are excellent and numerous.

Hughes, Donald James.
The neutron story. Doubleday Anchor Books, Garden City, 1959. 158 p.
Written in the straightforward manner of a scientific treatise, the story is a thrilling one, from the discovery of the particle in 1932, to fission in 1939, and atomic energy in 1942. Hughes, having recently written a book on neutrons for the professional physicist, has skillfully simplified it and embellished it with ample examples and analogies.

Humphreys, Richard F., and Beringer, Robert.
First principles of atomic physics. Harper, New York, 1950.
An introductory physics text for the student of the humanities or the social sciences.

Lapp, Ralph Eugene.
Atoms and people. Harper, New York, 1956.
Step by step, Lapp traces the story of the development of the theory of the chain reaction, the first pile, the first bomb, and finally the complete family of nuclear weapons.

Lapp, Ralph Eugene.
The new force; the story of atoms and people. Harper, New York, 1953.
Designed for a popular audience rather than only for the author's scientific colleagues, the book tells "the story of atoms and people" in a lucid and readily comprehensible manner.

The eyewitness accounts of many events of the last ten years are especially interesting and informing.

Semat, Henry.
Introduction to atomic and nuclear physics. 3rd ed., rev. and enl. Rinehart, New York, 1954.
An introductory textbook used in the instruction of undergraduate college students who have completed courses in basic physics and calculus.

NUCLEAR PHYSICS—FOR THE SCIENTIST

Eisenbud, Leonard, and Wigner, Eugene P.
Nuclear structure. Princeton University Press, 1958.
Originally prepared as a section for the *Handbook of Physics,* this small book provides a succinct description of the models and phenomena pertinent to an understanding of nuclear structure. A fine, brief survey of present attempts to understand the nucleus.

Friedlander, Gerhart, and Kennedy, Joseph W.
Nuclear and radiochemistry. Rev. version of *Introduction to radiochemistry.* Wiley, New York, 1955.
An introductory text primarily for advanced undergraduate and graduate students of chemistry. Treatment is more descriptive than mathematical, but the authors have assumed that the reader will be able to read graphs, solve algebraic equations, etc. The book is suitable for home reading by chemistry graduates who desire a grasp of the elementary basic knowledge of nuclear science and radiochemistry.

Frisch, Otto Robert, ed.
Nuclear handbook. Van Nostrand, Princeton, 1958.
Contains condensed and tabulated data which is needed in research and the practical application of nuclear science. Among the areas covered are particle accelerators, charged particles, X rays and gamma rays, neutrons, and ion chamber and counters.

Hoag, J. Barton.
Electron and nuclear physics. 3rd ed., rev. by S. A. Korff.
Van Nostrand, New York, 1948.
Chiefly for senior college and graduate students of physics, but
has also considerable historical and reference value for persons
trained in physics.

Hoisington, David B.
Nucleonics fundamentals. McGraw-Hill, New York, 1959.
A very broad coverage of the field of nucleonics. The treatment
of the subject matter is not highly mathematical; thus the work
is suited as a text for undergraduate survey courses, and as a
reference for graduate scientists and engineers interested in
learning something of the development and potentialities of
this field.

Littler, D. J., and Raffle, J. F.
Introduction to reactor physics. Published for the United
Kingdom Atomic Energy Authority. McGraw-Hill, New
York, 1955.
A well-balanced survey of pile theory. Should be very helpful
to those about to teach, or to be taught, the subject of Reactor
Physics. No mathematical knowledge required beyond the theory
of differential equations.

Martin, Frederick Samuel, and Miles, G. L.
Chemical processing of nuclear fuels. Academic Press, New
York, 1958.
Mainly a description of the chemistry of nuclear-fuel processing,
not the processing itself. Recommended to the science or engineering graduate who desires more information about the
basic chemistry of nuclear-fuel processing, and who does not
expect to find a discussion of the associated technology.

National Research Council Conference on Glossary of Terms
in Nuclear Science and Technology.
A glossary of terms in nuclear science and technology. American Society of Mechanical Engineers, New York, 1957.
189 p.

REACTORS AND POWER PLANTS—
FOR THE LAYMAN

Glasstone, Samuel.

Sourcebook on atomic energy. Van Nostrand, New York, 1950. 546 p.

Presents, in terms that such nonspecialist readers as journalists, teachers and industrial executives can understand, the historical development and a factual, reasonably detailed account of the current state of the subject.

REACTORS AND POWER PLANTS—
FOR THE TECHNICIAN

American Institute of Chemical Engineers.

Nuclear engineering. Part I. F. J. Van Antwerpen, editor and publisher, The Institute, New York, 1954. (Number 11 in its chemical engineering progress symposium series.)

The first of three volumes in the Chemical Engineering Progress Symposium Series, from the meeting on nuclear engineering sponsored by the American Institute of Chemical Engineers and the University of Michigan at Ann Arbor on June 20 to 25, 1954. Papers on reactor technology, materials of production, engineering research, engineering education, fuels, reactor statistics and reactor products—written by representatives of foreign countries and engineers from industry and government in the United States.

——Part II. F. J. Van Antwerpen, editor and publisher, The Institute, New York, 1954. (Number 12.)

Part II of the series. Papers on applications and uses of radioactive products, materials of reactor construction, nuclear power reactors, reactor-fuel refining and preparation, reactor technology, research and educational reactors, and separations technology.

——Part III. F. J. Van Antwerpen, editor, The Institute, New York, 1954. (Number 13.)

Part III of the series. Papers on applications and uses of radioactive products, education for nuclear engineers, nuclear power reactors, reactor-fuel refining and preparation, reactor technology, research and educational reactors, separations technology and the social impact of nuclear energy.

American Institute of Chemical Engineers. Nuclear Engineering Division Symposium on non-destructive tests in the field of nuclear energy. American Society for Testing Materials, Philadelphia, 1958. (ASTM special technical publication, No. 223.)

Developments in ultrasonic and eddy current test procedures and applications made in the inspection of castings, tubing, components, and clad and unclad fuel elements.

Bonilla, Charles F., ed.
Nuclear engineering. McGraw-Hill, New York, 1957.

Written by 12 experts in various fields of engineering and science, this reference work gives the basic principles of the main engineering disciplines involved in the design of nuclear reactor cores and power plants. In each of the 12 fields, the fundamentals are given briefly and clearly with enough illustrations and advanced specific analyses so that the book is valuable to the working design engineer as well as to the student.

Glasstone, Samuel.
Principles of nuclear reactor engineering. Van Nostrand, New York, 1955. 861 p.

A broad survey of the current state of reactor theory and engineering design is presented, except that knowledge not yet declassified is not included. No previous acquaintance with nuclear physics or reactor design has been assumed; on the other hand the book is addressed to readers with substantial education in engineering.

Hausner, Henry Herman, and Schumar, James F., eds.
Nuclear fuel elements. Reinhold, New York, 1959.

Papers presented at the First International Symposium on Nuclear Fuel Elements held at Columbia University in January, 1959. First-hand information from scientists in the United States and European countries who have worked on the development, design and fabrication of fuel elements.

Hurst, R., and McLain, S., eds.
  Technology and engineering . . . McGraw-Hill, New York,
  1956.

  A compilation of selected important Geneva papers, along with
  several new ones on the general subject of coolant and moderator technology. Particularly useful to the worker in this field
  who does not have the corresponding Geneva volumes.

National Research Council Conference on Glossary of Terms
in Nuclear Science and Technology.
  A glossary of terms in nuclear science and technology. American Society of Mechanical Engineers, New York, 1957.
  189 p.

Nucleonics (periodical).
  *Handbook of new nuclear techniques, providing the latest
  experience in nuclear energy applications.* McGraw-Hill,
  New York, 1953.

  Compiled from articles which appeared in *Nucleonics Magazine.*
  The subject matter includes nuclear engineering and reactor
  technology, instrumentation, chemistry, medical and biological
  effects of radiation, uses of radioisotopes, and physics and provides experience in nuclear energy applications affecting the
  interests of electrical engineers, metallurgists, chemists, chemical
  engineers, electronic specialists, scientists, physicists, biologists,
  radiobiologists and industrial plant managers.

Schultz, Mortimer A.
  Control of nuclear reactors and power plants. McGraw-Hill,
  New York, 1955.

  Suitable for use as a text in graduate courses and as self-instruc-
  tion for graduate engineers who are making their first acquaintance with the control of nuclear reactors. The control of nuclear
  reactors is studied here as a problem in control-system design
  rather than as a problem in reactor engineering.

Schwenk, Henry C., and Shannon, Robert H.
  Nuclear power engineering. McGraw-Hill, New York, 1957.
  This book, planned for engineers, technicians and executives
  concerned with practical power development, gives an explana-

tion of the design, construction and operation of nuclear power plants.

Thompson, A. Stanley, and Rodgers, Oliver E.
Thermal power from nuclear reactors. Wiley, New York, 1956.
An authoritative book on the engineering of nuclear reactors designed for the production of power, primarily an analytical treatment. In addition to the engineering topics, some background topics in physics are covered also.

OTHER USES OF RADIOACTIVITY

Bradford, John R., ed.
Radioisotopes in industry. Reinhold, New York, 1953.
Information on the availability, potential applications and manipulation of radioactive isotopes in measurement, inspection and research. Contains valuable information for all who are beginning to use radioactive isotopes or who are interested in their industrial applications.

Calvin, Melvin (and others).
Isotopic carbon; techniques in its measurement and chemical manipulation. Wiley, New York, 1949.
A reference book and laboratory manual for the use of scientists and technicians in laboratory procedures.

Chase, Grafton D.
Principles of radioisotope methodology. Burgess, Minneapolis, 1959.
Written primarily for the beginner in the field of radioisotopes. A laboratory manual rather than a treatise on current theory. Fundamental theory is covered enough to satisfy the need for an understanding of the experiments involved.

Conference on Isotope Techniques, Oxford, 1951.
Radioisotopes techniques; V.2: Industrial and allied research applications. H. M. Stationery Office, London, 1952.
The purpose of the Isotope Techniques Conference, held at Oxford, July 16-20, 1951, was to assemble those who were using radioisotopes in various fields to promote discussion and to establish liaison. Ninety-eight papers were presented.

Glascock, Raymond.
Labelled atoms; the use of radioactive and stable isotopes in biology and medicine. Sigma, London, 1951.
> Recommended not only to the layman interested in acquiring a surer knowledge of what is behind press releases about the beneficial effects of isotopes and atomic energy, but also to scientists whose interests lie outside this field and who can spend only a limited time in acquiring familiarity with applied isotopy.

Guest, Gordon Hamilton.
Radioisotopes; industrial applications. Pitman, New York, 1951.
> Explains the properties of radioisotopes in very simple terms and points out their possible uses in industry. Should be easily understood by persons who have had no special training in radiochemistry. A concise, readable collection of background information for the layman or the industrialist who is considering the use of radioisotopes in his business.

Libby, Willard F.
Radiocarbon dating. 2nd ed. University of Chicago Press, 1955.
> The principles and techniques of estimating the ages of organic materials, especially artifacts of archaeological interest, by measuring their radioactive carbon contents.

Rochlin, Robert S., and Schultz, Warner W.
Radioisotopes for industry. Reinhold, New York, 1959.
> Applications of radioisotopes in industry specifically described, and many new uses suggested. Sufficient material is included so that the reader can project the examples into his own needs. In addition, the authors discuss safety, handling facilities and setup costs.

SAFETY, CONTROL AND HAZARD

American Institute of Chemical Engineers. *Nuclear Engineering.* Part IV. F. J. Van Antwerpen, editor and publisher, The Institute, New York, 1956. 206 p.
> Part IV of the series. Papers on safety measures and waste disposal.

Nucleonics (periodical).

Handbook of new nuclear techniques, providing the latest experience in nuclear energy applications. McGraw-Hill, New York, 1953.

Compiled from articles which appeared in *Nucleonics Magazine*. The subject matter includes nuclear engineering and reactor technology, instrumentation, chemistry, medical and biological effects of radiation, uses of radioisotopes, and physics and provides experience in nuclear energy applications affecting the interests of electrical engineers, metallurgists, chemists, chemical engineers, electronic specialists, scientists, physicists, biologists, radiobiologists and industrial plant managers.

Price, William James.

Nuclear radiation detection. McGraw-Hill, New York, 1958.

Aimed at those interested in acquiring the basic information on radiation detectors in use at the present time.

Shamos, Morris H., and Roth, Sidney G., eds.

Industrial and safety problems of nuclear technology. Harper, New York, 1950.

The treatment is designed for the layman; it covers non-military uses of atomic energy in industry, agriculture and medicine. Prepared for a three-day conference sponsored by the Atomic Energy Commission and New York University's Division of General Education.

Annotations of the books in the bibliography were compiled from *Technical Book Review Index* published by the Special Libraries Association, *Book Review Digest* published by the H. W. Wilson Company, and R. R. Hawkins' *Scientific, Medical, and Technical Books Published in the United States of America.*

INDEX